József Marx

FATELESS – A BOOK OF THE FILM

Lajos Koltai's film
based on the novel by Nobel Laureate Imre Kertész

József Marx

FATELESS – A BOOK OF THE FILM

Lajos Koltai's film
based on the novel by Nobel Laureate Imre Kertész

(handwritten dedication and signatures)

2007. 09. 08.
L. A.

VINCE BOOKS

Photographs of *Fateless* by Buda Gulyás

© József Marx, 2005

© Vince Books, 2005

Published in 2005 by Vince Books
A member of the Association of Hungarian Book Publishers and Book Distributors
(1027 Budapest, Margit körút 64/b)
Telephone: (36-1) 375-7288 Fax: (36-1) 202-7145

www.vincekiado.hu

The Director of Vince Books is responsible for publishing
Editor in Charge: Katalin Sebes
Designed by Tünde Kálmán
Layout by Erzsi Jeges
Picture Production by Austral Co., Karina Leitner

Printed by Dürer Printing House, Gyula
Managing Director: András Megyik

ISBN 963 9552 53 4

Translated by Katalin Rácz
Translation revised by Bob Dent
English Translation © Katalin Rácz, 2005

Front cover photograph by Buda Gulyás
Back cover photograph by Eszter Gordon

CONTENTS

LAJOS KOLTAI'S STORY

A YOUNG PAIR OF EYES

"Sutyi is just like he was at the entrance examination." Sutyi is the nickname of Lajos Koltai, and the words are from the ninety-year-old György Illés, the beloved master of five-six generations of Hungarian cameramen.[1] He explained what he meant. If he looks Lajos Koltai in the eye, which he often does these days, the same young pair of eyes looks back at him without having lost their animated interest and merry spirit.

"He is still thinking hard of new lighting effects as he did when he was my assistant cameraman in *The Ants' Nest*. Have a look how many of us have become uninterested, broken down and have left the profession, even if they have had no reason to do so. He will never stop."

It is good to hear such a long-term prediction at the special time when the disciple, at the peak of a cinematographer's career, makes his debut as a director.

"Lajos Koltai is going to direct," many whispered in professional circles, but not like as if an extraordinary piece of news were being spread. There are examples of noted cameramen occupying the director's chair for a while. Although a long time ago, Eisenstein's constant cinematographer, the especially gifted Eduard Tisse presented himself as a director, and so did Sven Nykvist, Ingmar Bergman's colleague, in the not so distant past. Nevertheless, it is a noteworthy event when an 'artist of light' sits in the rather shaky chair of the beginner director. He must surely know that there will be a number of people who will want to work with him if the film is a success, but should it fail he will be left alone, as if stranded on a desert island.

Lajos Koltai's new career can be seen as part of a story which carries sufficient meaning in itself to enable the intuitive or conscious viewer to understand the work of art as a whole. If we approach the work by outlining the artist's story retrospectively, we will proceed completely in the spirit of the directors of the French Nouvelle Vague. From the contemporary cinematography, mockingly called 'daddy's movies', the master Alfred Hitchcock, the 'great survivor', was the only one respected by the French young. That was not by chance. He was wise without displaying the slightest hint of conceit. He said that a film represented the unity of maker, the film and the audience. Should just one member of the unit fail there will be no film. Of course, they exist, but here we are not interested in that type of ready made 'product' which lacks personality. It is enough if our vision is filled by *Fateless* and not only (or primarily) by Imre Kertész's novel and the Nobel Prize, but the somewhat slight absurdity signalled by the subtitle of this book: *Lajos Koltai's film…* What is this? If we must give a brief answer, it is the first work directed by an undeterred young film maker.[2]

---

[1] For those to whom this nickname diminutive of 'stripling' or 'youngster' does not say much, let me quote the dictionary, which says that it originally means 'a swishing tree, a young branch', since it comes from the verb 'to give a swishing sound'. Let this be the deeper meaning of Lajos Koltai's name. It was his father, also called Lajos, who gave him this name when he was three years old.

[2] Why use the adjective undeterred? I thus characterised Lajos Koltai exactly twenty-five years ago when he began working with István Szabó. I have had no reason since to withdraw the adjective

THE YOUNG DOG

Two famous writings from the beginning of the1940s can be selected to provide literary and psychological support for determining the portraits of film directors. One is a short story by Sartre, *The Childhood of a Leader*, while the other is Dylan Thomas's autobiographical short stories, *Portrait of the Artist as a Young Dog*. With vitriolic sharpness Sartre depicted the young bourgeois hero who, in the end, chooses the worst way in his search for identity – he is consumed by the desire for power and becomes rooted in an environment which feeds this desire. In contrast, Dylan Thomas's stories use images and the precise description of objects and people to recall with irony and understanding the Welsh adolescent who has not yet thought of poetry becoming his most natural habitat. The adolescent is living and observing as if these two activities had some purpose, although he himself does not yet know what the purpose may be. However, the volume clearly suggests that the great poems, which entirely renewed Anglo-Saxon poetry, would not have been written without the 'young dog's' existence.

These two types of behaviour reflect two types of choice. One grasps reality violently, wanting to reshape it to its own image, the other would rather like to understand it with an affectionate attitude usually reserved for our loved ones.

As a 'young dog', Lajos Koltai can be characterised by affectionate relationships. This was not accidental – he was the child of not only his optimistic parents but also the country, as it emerged from the hell of war with optimism. He was born on 2 April 1946, the son of Lajos Koltai and Valéria Hufnágel, the beautiful daughter of a furrier, two days before the first anniversary of the country's liberation, when parties still competed for power and a coalition government directed the difficult job of rebuilding the country. The conditions were, of course, hard. Budapest was in ruins, the bridges crossing the Danube hung mangled and distorted in the murky river and people were only beginning to realise the losses. There was no family without someone who had died, disappeared or been taken prisoner. Despite all this, there was a heroic feeling of

The young Lajos Koltai in 1950 with his father, also Lajos, his mother, Valéria Hufnágel, and his sister, Bea

restarting anew, reflected in Géza Radványi's *Somewhere in Europe*, the first post-war Hungarian film to attract significant international attention. Then the sky darkened over Hungary. In the shadow of the Soviet occupying forces a one-party system was formed in 1949. The Communist Party dealt a merciless blow to its domestic opponents, and there began the reign of Mátyás Rákosi, 'the wise leader of the country'. Rákosi recognised only one idea as redeeming – his own. Europe was divided by two spheres of interest. The borders became impenetrable, not only by the Iron Curtain in its physical sense.

Koltai's family sheltered the 'young dog' from the rough effects of the environment, as had been an unwritten law in bringing up children in Hungary for centuries. It used to be called 'dual education' – schools, the outside world taught something different from that of the family. The former promoted incomprehensible values and unachievable aims, the latter gave an example of staunch survival. It was pure survival which mattered most for the majority in this part of Europe. Families considered it a matter of course that children must be brought up so that they would feel good under the generally bad circumstances. But not by deception – they did not label evil as good, rather families were adamant to find a tiny event, object or encouraging smile, which they could hand over to their offspring as a bright recompense against the world of evil. 'Happy childhood' is not an unknown notion even in dictatorships. Of course,

Bea and Lajos on the Fishermen's Bastion in 1952

we should avoid the mistake of evaluating every motion of Koltai's biography as if everything were pointing in the direction of *Fateless*. Nevertheless, it could be justly said that there were numerous moments in the post-war childhood of Lajos Koltai when a gap appeared between the softness of a child's view and the reality filling adults with fear, when the child proved to be more understanding about reality than his parents, who, in turn, considered this greater understanding as a triumph of their education.

Lajos Koltai was born, with the help of a midwife, at home in Szentendre Road on the Buda side of the Hungarian capital, which lies on the two banks of the river Danube. The scene of his life was Old Buda, the Ofenbuda of former Swabian vine-growers, but this was not that world which left the first traces in his memory. The poor family without prospects (the father was dismissed from his jobs from time to time by every system) left their small home in the summers and moved to have their holiday by the other big Hungarian river, the Tisza. The children, Lajos and his elder sister Bea, received the greatest holiday present with the move, even when they were already at school. The 'outpost' was offered by their paternal grandfather Kopper,

Travelling to Tiszadob; grandfather Kopper can be seen behind the mother

who was pensioned off from his 'high office' at the end of the 1940s (he worked as a meter reader for the Electricity Board) and his wife, grandmother Porkoláb, who, fearing starvation, persuaded her husband to move to the country. From there grandfather kept sending letters constantly asking for help. "My son, we are starving here. Send us two hundred forints." Anyway, it was only the summer that mattered to the child. The worn trench coat, beret and patched up tracksuit bottom could be taken off and they could get ready.

At that time this type of holiday was not called village tourism since it involved necessity rather than free choice. However, the children were not aware of this and were happy to set up at their grandparents' place, where half the village were relatives because of the Porkolábs in Tiszadob, a village between the Tisza and one of its dead branches, far from Budapest. Even the journey was an adventure. Why would they mind while the horse and cart was jouncing from the railway station to the village that they were in Szabolcs, the poorest county in Hungary, bordering Ukraine on one side and Romania on the other. True, there were also Hungarians living across the border, but at the time only among very close friends would adults dare to curse the borders drawn up as a result of World War I. The children may have sensed the world by sudden outbursts of anger, while they learnt about fantastic novelties. For example, what a pig was like, how a cat purred and how a dog can be stroked, what villagers called a pit, a sweet corn store, what the summer kitchen was and what the 'best room' represented with its two windows

Lajos Koltai in the fifth year of primary school in 1957 (middle row, far right)

overlooking the street, where one was allowed to enter only on very rare occasions. They also saw a mansion.

The mansion of Gyula Andrássy, a former Hungarian prime minister noted for his devotion to Queen Elisabeth, was designed in the 1880s by one of the most renowned Hungarian architects, Ignác Alpár. The building, with its four entrances, twelve towers, fifty-two rooms and as many windows as there are days in the year, reminds the visitor of the Loire valley. The spectacle was, of course, depressing at the beginning of the 1950s. Just like the most beautiful avenues (Andrássy Avenue in Budapest was changed to Stalin Avenue), the mansion went to ruin. But even in its devastated condition, with its famous park overgrown, it was a child's paradise.

Naturally the river Tisza was the real spectacle in Tiszadob. The locals were proud to mention that here at the gateway of the Tisza floods the 'greatest Hungarian', Count István Széchenyi, dug the first sod to start the massive work of regulating the river. Cranes built mill-wheel sized nests in the woods of the flood plains and the velvety waters of the dead branches gave themselves to long bathing.

The 'young dog's' memory preserved the line of poplars along the river bank and passed it on to the adult film maker. The image was a picture seen as an apparition at the border of life and death. As it happened the bathing adults missed the child wading in the water after them. He was lucky to be seen by a woman on the bank, who due to fright was able to shout only "the child!". Luck was further enhanced by the fact that on that day the child was wearing red swimming trunks. The father saw them in the water and scooped up his unconscious son, who, as the last flash of his consciousness, already from under the water caught sight of the poplars battling with the sky. The parents were truly frightened, but Lajos Koltai learnt about the reason for the fright only as an adult. A child had already died in the family. He was 'only' the third. The younger of his two sisters, Mártika, while still a baby caught a cold and died on 5 December 1944. There was no medical help in the shelter where Budapest residents who were not able to leave the capital before the Russian siege lived like moles amidst continuous bombing.

The adults considered Lajos to be skinny, which increased their fright. He did not have the build of a gymnast later, although he was the first in Hungary who took the camera in the hand, which would not have been a minor deed even for a sporting performance. Unlike his peers, he liked doing things which required thinking, especially after their holidays in Tiszadob had finished. Grandmother Porkoláb died in 1955 and the grandfather was brought up to Budapest together with his furniture in a lorry. The family was able to feel well-off for some time with the forty thousand forints from the sale of the Tiszadob house.

Grandfather loved his grandson very much, looked after him and, for example, revealed the secrets of chess. Otherwise, grandfather was regarded as an artist in the family, since he often played the singing-dancing comedian in the performances of the Tabán amateur theatre group. The child was proud of his grandfather who dressed in strange clothes and was enthusiastically applauded by the audience. An operetta of the 1920s, the *Woman of Kisses* by Béla Zerkovitz, was one performance greeted with boisterous acclaim.

Several years, the years at primary school and the first years at secondary school, passed by. The child's life unfolded within narrow boundaries. The family lived next door to the school. Lajos Koltai's mother could watch her son going to school from the kitchen window. A few images of the 1950s have remained in the memory of the 'young dog', who tolerated with a smile the adults constantly teasing him. He can still remember scenes quite 'free of politics', like his mother and grandmother leaning over the Singer sewing machine at home, its foot pedal providing the power, with only the lamp of the machine casting a light on them in the dawn semi-darkness. Clients would bring their dresses for alterations, asking his mother 'to perform a miracle'. She was able to do that. For example, it was never obvious that her son's winter coat had already served several seasons as his sister's coat.

As a grown man, he remembers the image of the fair at Old Buda most vividly. Vendors and stall-holders set up their tents all the way from the school to the gasworks. There was a lot to see, but the child's attention was mostly attracted by the swing boats in constant movement. He actually became 'swing addicted'. When he was able to scrape together fifty fillers he had a ride as a heavenly joy. On one occasion he even stole fifty fillers from his parents, but he was not clever. He hid the money from his mother, who suddenly turned up, his fist in his pocket, but forgot that his shorts had just an opening without a real pocket. Discovery was followed by punishment and the often heard parental complaint that nothing would become of the child – a man at the swings perhaps. He did not make progress with learning to play the piano. His parents did not understand why he sat down to the instrument only if threatened. He, of course, knew. If he failed to hold his hands over the keys as if he were holding an apple, the piano teacher would hit them with a ruler.

This is not the place to write about historical events, although it was quite an experience in 1956 when a Soviet tank turned into the street and at the corner was immediately shot at by revolutionaries. As in 1944-45, the family survived the fierce shooting in the cellar (there were Soviet barracks nearby). The child was rather surprised at the neighbours taking everything movable out of the tank, such that the cellar was filled with tanks seats.

What may really interest the reader is to recognise the moment when divine inspiration appeared in the director-cameraman's head making him proclaim: "I'll be a film maker!" Unfortunately, potential expectations regarding this moment must be dispelled. During Lajos Koltai's childhood and youth events turned out in such a way that he realised and was not surprised that he was *already* committed to cinematography. No doubt he was impressed when he first saw a camera. While at school, he was an extra in László Nádasy's *Raid* (1958), a film destined to be forgotten. He is the child at the Eastern Railway Station walking with a large water jug behind the two great actors of the time, János Görbe and Ádám Szirtes. However, let us not think that being an extra was to be a determining experience. It is not known whether his desire to act was due to budding film talent or the natural exhibitionism of adolescence. He could not excel with outstanding sports performance and he was not good at ordering people around, thus he was left with smart thinking, the pleasant articulation of well-thought ideas and love. There was no anxiety when he had to stand up before an audience and he recited poems as if they were his own thoughts, which he *interpreted* together with his literature teacher.

There was a film club in his secondary grammar school, which was named after Sándor Körösi Csoma, the explorer of Tibet during Hungary's Reform Age. It was a dual-language school, where Russian was used in teaching along with Hungarian, the former being replaced by German today. In retrospect, the film club seems to have been a fantastic coincidence, but it is not entirely so. The fact that there was a film club in the 'Körösi', almost in the suburbs of the capital, indicates that the social role of cinema was rising in Hungary. The indisputable fact that modern Hungarian film had managed to enter the vanguard of European cinema had seeped through the old walls of the school. Notwithstanding the debates of the time, *Cantata* by Miklós Jancsó and *Current* by István Gaál in 1963, and *The Age of Daydreaming* by István Szabó in the next year signalled that Hungarian films were respected internationally. Hungarian film makers were 'good brands' at home, too. Yet since cinematography was considered a closed profession in Hungary, as elsewhere, it can be added that whoever wanted to be a film maker also needed luck. However, to be lucky was not enough on its own, one had to grasp the smallest chance. For example, it was Lajos Koltai's idea to have the film club. He also begged for leftover negatives from the television studios and then it seemed to be a golden opportunity when his sister's boyfriend, who was interested in film, lent him his spring-operated camera for the weekends. He must have thought that at least the boy would not be under their feet. But it was really fate which tested what he could make of the rudimentary Bolex camera. Would he handle it with as much love as a cameraman or regard it as a disposable toy like the majority of children?

Árpád Burza first handed Lajos Koltai the camera and thought the event worth taking

ON BECOMING
A CAMERAMAN

A cameraman grasps reality with both hands. His is not a theoretical profession. He uses light, a reel and a camera – they are not external faculties. A cameraman not only learns but *knows* that the camera penetrates reality, just like a surgeon's scalpel. An aesthete's virtual reality is real for him; after all, a task is not only to be imagined but also to be undertaken. Briefly, a camera has to be taken in hand and the start button must be pushed. The great magic, editing, happens after the developing process, which itself is full of surprises (amateur photographers know what a difference there can be between the picture through the view-finder and the developed photo). Editing constructs a new reality from the existing frames.

Lajos Koltai became a leading personality in the school amateur film club, since from among short films on school experiences and first love his short feature *The Fence* was awarded a festival prize and the jury of amateur films also mentioned his *Improvisations*. He was especially pleased to hear the verbal appraisal because when he was looking for someone for the leading role he was recommended a girl

from the legendary second-hand bookshop, since disappeared, in Váci Street in the city centre. The girl's name was Katalin Bordás whom he managed to talk into accepting the role. (Why was the jury's appraisal important? We will see later.)

Receiving the prize was a fantastic event in the secondary school pupil's life, for otherwise the school years left only dark memories with him. They were literally dark. The poorly lit gymnasium, where he would recite a poem at school ceremonies, became unforgettable.

The prize was a gift from the goddess of fortune but, as we know, amateur festival winners seldom become

Facing college (1965)

professionals. It also requires the family to accept what career is chosen. Lajos Koltai did not have to argue with his parents because of an artistic career. His sister had already paved the way – she wanted to become a theatre director and it was already the third round of entrance examinations when the college gate closed for her. The father, who was a radio enthusiast, on the side sending in radio reports on economic matters, got his daughter to work for Hungarian television as a sort of 'dog's body'.[3] So it was not accidental that Lajos Koltai began to work as an extra for the television. The jobs in front of the camera had a strong influence on the young man. For example, László Marton, only three months his senior, was working as an extra with him in one of the productions. Marton would become a theatre director and is currently the chief director-manager of the Variety Theatre in Budapest. Those roles presumably also taught him how to approach a boss and how to make a proposal in an appropriate way. In addition, confidence was certainly needed after graduating from the grammar school. Thus he simply went in

[3] Beáta Koltay became the director of hundreds of television programmes after she had graduated from Budapest University's Faculty of Humanities with two majors, Hungarian literature and public education. One of her most noted directions involved the original appearance of actress Ildikó Kishonti, which was shown in many countries of the world. In 1967 she married Miklós Bíró, the chief cameraman of HTV.

to the TV headquarters and stood in front of the all-powerful chief producer's secretary. He asked her to take into consideration his past in amateur films and his 'practice' in studio work. This hair-raising impertinence moved Éva Kecskés (Koltai remembers her name even after nearly four decades), and she assigned the smart young man to cameraman Árpád Burza in the crew of the *Newsreel*.

The young man rose quickly on the professional ladder. From a second assistant cameraman he became first assistant, even taking the camera in hand such that while watching the evening news he could say: "I took that picture!" That undoubtedly helped a person's self-confidence. The rising 'career', of course, did not just happen. Hard work, observation and an elementary desire to learn were all in the background – in brief, there was his character. As well as the profession he continued to 'learn' the double view of the world. There was an incredibly large gap between the opinion of the crew and the presenter's comments when the *Newsreel* had to report on the removal of Soviet party secretary Khrushchev in October 1964, or the demolition of the National Theatre in Blaha Lujza Square in March 1965. The *Newsreel* production team often did not even believe itself.

COLLEGE

The year spent in the television encouraged Koltai to apply to the College of Drama and Cinematography. One of the members of the examination board was István Szabó, who, in a pleasant surprise, asked the applicant about the film *Fence*. They had an enjoyable conversation while the others, who were unfamiliar with the seemingly notable amateur film, listened intently.

The Hungarian College (today University) of Drama and Cinematography has always been a noted, internationally famous institution. Naturally, its fame was created by its later well-known students, whose lion's claws could be seen through the holes in their socks already as students, to quote the favourite metaphor of István Szőts, the neo-realist forerunner of Hungarian film. Cinematography had been taught in the college since 1945 and there was not a year when a head of the cinematography faculty did not modify the curriculum. In the years when Lajos Koltai attended the college, the director János Herskó was the deputy principal and the cinematography boss. What he wanted to introduce became law. For example, he had the idea of getting applicants who had already had some experience, some 'past', namely, had graduated from another university. That was how Lívia Gyarmathy and Sándor Simó, and later Géza Böszörményi began the college in 1961 and 1964 respectively. All three of them were chemical engineers.[4] In 1965 this programme was modified – all is well with mature people taking the lead, but what is going to happen to young people with a new approach? Those young people were meant to be represented by Gyula Gazdag, born in 1947, and Lajos

---

[4] János Herskó's approach was justified by his pupils' first, successful films (almost the best in their careers), like Lívia Gyarmathy's film, *Do you know "Sunday-Monday"?* (1969) and Géza Böszörményi's *Birdies* (1970). Both represented early films in the line of grotesque pictures of Hungarian cinema.

Koltai. Incidentally, this programme worked well, since Gazdag's first film, *Whistling Cobblestone* (1971), was a promising start. The programme also contained the very important point that applicants were admitted to do director-cameraman courses, i.e. *cinematography*, and to specialise after the second year. Therefore Lajos Koltai's course tutor was not a cameraman but a director, the master Félix Máriássy, who wisely fostered István Szabó's generation.

The five years at the college for Lajos Koltai was as if someone had paid him for all the rounds on the swing-boat of his childhood. He devoured all information from eight in the morning to eight in the evening. He loved Éva Szőllősy's lectures on art history. The legendary lecturer taught generations how to analyse pictures, the history of styles and the love of art. He was also taught by Géza Hegedüs, the writer who was at home in any language or style, and whose lectures on the history of literature were free of pedantry. The comparison with the swing-boat is valid in as much as there were also low points. For example, the examination film *The*

"My first roll of film." The materiality of the socio-photo made at the photographic exhibition and the impressionist floating of the window cleaner at the Southern Railway Station convinced the lecturers of the candidate's talent

Seventh Day directed and filmed at the end of the first year showed a Csepel metal worker's monotonous days, his commuting between the large factory regarded as the citadel of socialist industry and his village house, of which only the base was properly built. There was a shot of a kitchen table with numerous marks grooved by decades. Hopelessness was palpable and this shot then ran into the 'triumphant' sparkles of the foundry. The student did not yet know that his teachers would interpret it as a symbol. The principal regarded the 13-minute black and white examination film as a direct slander on the proletarian way of life. It became a matter of chance. The ambitious young man would have been immediately 'filtered out', to employ the expression used at the college, if, for example, Éva Szőllősy and Ibolya Fövény, who taught aesthetics, had not come to his aid. Women are always braver. The male lecturers were absolutely silent. They knew why they did not enter into confrontation. On several occasions they had themselves experienced what it meant when political criticism was raised by the higher authority concerning a film. The film *The Round-up* by Miklós Jancsó shown on 6 January 1966 was their most recent experience. Critical arrows poured on the film, since it was undeniably a metaphor for the retribution after the 1956 revolution.

Mention of *The Round-up* is important as illustration of the fact that those five years Lajos Koltai spent at the College witnessed the rising period of Hungarian film. Then everyone really felt in control and the political elite realised that films could create the so much desired legitimacy abroad and therefore it was willing to grant 'concessions'. Consequently, college students could rightly think that the world can be conquered. The Béla Balázs Studio, the self-governing studio of college students and young directors was functioning at the beginning of the 1960s, but it was only at the end of the decade when the conditions were right for the studio to produce a full-length feature film. The film *Agitators* by Dezső Magyar was also Lajos Koltai's diploma film. There was a steeply rising way to the work. Koltai first had to specialise and went in for the profession of cameraman without thinking. He may have taken into consideration that Gyula Gazdag, his 'student pair' (the tutorial group was divided into pairs as practice for creative cooperation), wanted to become a director[5] and therefore cinematography was 'left' for him. Naturally, most important for him was that this profession was closer to his character, his tactile sensitivity, which quality was independent of the ideological disputes unfolding as a

Cinematographic practice in the studio of the College with Gyula Gazdag

[5] Gyula Gazdag directed and Lajos Koltai filmed the 6-minute examination film *The Holiday* (1966). They also made the 19-minute examination film *Prelude* in the same year.

pretext around a film's content. He loved the laboratory situation, the moment when in the projection room viewing the rushes it was possible to check whether the pictorial idea had come true or a so-far unrecognised feature of the material, the light or the camera had added new angles (or rather in most cases ruined) the intense work of days.

The second stage of the road leading to the diploma film was made possible by the best virtue of the college – it let students learn from each other. An avant-garde circle was formed around Dezső Magyar and Gábor Bódy when the unusually long, 40 minute examination film *Three Girls* (1968) was made. The inner circle included György (Georg) Pintér, István Dárday and Éva Schulze. Lajos Koltai was also invited along. He was happy to get involved and squeezed out whatever was possible from the 16mm film and the inadequate technology. As a gesture of appreciation, Dezső Magyar asked him to be the cameraman for the film which reconstructed the 1918-19 intellectuals' disputes on the necessity and methodology of the revolution, based on the novel *Optimists* by Ervin Sinkó and **on** the memories of the noted figures of the communist movement (György Lukács and Mrs Tibor Szamuely). Although the name of then camera genius of the college, Lajos Horváth, was mentioned, the film *Three Girls* was a good reference for the experimenting director, who thought that 'two was too many'. The cast, Gábor Bódy, László Földes (Hobó), László Bertalan, Tamás Szentjóby, Péter Dobai, Árpád Ajtony, Gábor Révai, György Cserhalmi, Sándor Oszter, András Kozák and Márk Zala made up a peculiar medley. The 'civilians', a director, poet, pop singer, philosopher, writer, and the would-be actors had to forget their professions. They did not act or live through but represented the pure critical mind according to their intentions and independently of the story. They represented the criticism against the ideology which existed during so-called socialism. The film was shot in a hotel in the town of Pécs, especially opened for the crew. To be constantly together with the others was like a special university course for Lajos Koltai. He had to realise that it was not enough to contemplate reality only through a lens. He must also keep his other eye open. He was already aware when half or two-thirds of the film had been shot that it would not be shown

Shooting *Silent Night* (1967). From left to right: Lajos Koltai, András Kern, the director-teacher Félix Máriássy, Nándor Tomanek and Tamás Farkas

The first long feature; Gábor Bódy performing in the film *Agitators* (1969)

to the public, but this did not distress him, rather it made him defiant. The idea was that the camera and the lighting should not disturb the improvisation, either in sound or movement. Therefore he used natural lighting, which the characters could freely move in. Koltai was able to work without any restrictions since he was only asked to make the pictures in a documentary style. The censors qualified the film as 'oppositional' until 1985 and it was only then that the public was able to view it. Nevertheless, even today the reality of the images can enthral the viewer.

AT WORK

The profession, however, took notice of the young cameraman. Koltai joined the Hungarian Film Company in 1970 and, as was usual at the time, he began at the bottom. He could not protest if he was assigned as an assistant cameraman in a production despite his degree. Koltai agreed since he was wise enough to know that he was not yet a real cameraman, although he had already made a feature film. However, the most respected cameraman, György Illés, picked him to be his colleague, which sweetened the possible bitterness of the assignment. They shot together in 1970 and 1971, and in particular the time spent beside Zoltán Fábri, the outstanding personality of Hungarian film, was really productive.

Koltai participated in the feats of lighting in the film *The Ants' Nest* (1971). Only two lights were on for a night scene being shot in the studio and the young assistant cameraman suggested that they turned off one, reaching the possible limits of the then used Kodak colour negative. Illés first sent him to hell (of course using a more literal expression), but he let him do it and later in the projecting room they were both pleased with the strong emotional effect of the scene.

The young ones did not really consider the way *The Ants' Nest* was made – from the script to the method of direction – as their 'guiding trend'. However, Koltai did not mind. He stored the experience gained with the film for 'better times', and in his independent work he became one of the core members of the innovative new generation. What did that mean at the beginning of the 1970s? The young ones wanted to do away with the quasi-reality of films and provide the viewer with the full illusion of reality. On the one hand, in documentaries they got rid of the way feature films were structured, while on the other, in feature films they said good-bye to the 'folding-unfolding' composition. They sought for images of reality as opposed to 'polished' pictures, and not colours but the atmosphere of a scene became most important for them. In effect, they waged war against colour; black and white became their ideal since they regarded that as the source of austerity rather than 'life like' colours. Some directors were especially displeased with the young declaring that they would approach a film without any preconceptions because the story must roll itself forward and arrive at an end result according to its own logic. The opponents' interpretation was that the young folk did not really know what they wanted, and without sparing time or resources were simply waiting for something to land on their plate.

When Koltai got to the film studios the atmosphere was by no means peaceful. It was the time when János Herskó had left the team of those already at the film studios and the college students who had gathered around him (with the expression of the time, he left the country illegally), and the struggle for the redistribution of film studio facilities had begun. Looking at matters from below, it was a bit different. The otherwise petty battles seemed to be the contest of the gods on Mount Olympus for Lajos Koltai, who did not wonder that neither side wanted the beginner cameraman badly. It did not matter – he did what he had to. The Béla Balázs Studio provided him with work. He was the cameraman for *Honeymoons*, a 38-minute report film, and he also worked in the Report and Documentary Studios of Mafilm, where together with an experienced colleague, István Zöldi, he shot a noted short, *Indecent Photographs*, directed by Géza Böszörményi. However, the 'great task' found Lajos Koltai again in the Béla Balázs Studio. During the shooting of *The Ants' Nest*, the actress Mari Törőcsik told him that Gyula Maár had the opportunity to make a full-length feature film based on his own script and that Ferenc Grunwalsky, Maár's permanent colleague, had recommended him as the cameraman. Koltai was overjoyed since he knew well that Maár was *not* a documentarist.

Cameraman in *The Ants' Nest* (1971). In the foreground Zoltán Fábri, the director; the one checking the clouds is the master, György Illés

With Gyula Maár when making *The Press* (1971)

As the shooting of *The Press* proceeded (it was filmed on 35mm negative, which filled him with special pleasure), Koltai saw it ever so clearly that the film, a Jancsó-like parable of power and obedience, would be unlikely to get a distribution licence from the censors. Yet it did not disappoint him. He observed how devotedly the exceptional actress Mari Törőcsik served the film and he did not want to lag behind her in his commitment. Due to the unfiltered lights everything had a sharp shadow, thus the pictures received a graphic character. The camera got tuned to the sorrowful feeling of enclosure and was sometimes looking for a way out of the suffocating world with unexpected movements.

News of the film spread and many in the profession wanted to try out the 'new young man'. It was not an impossible task since to make a documentary was almost fashionable at the beginning of the 1970s. These films, rarely longer than 20 minutes, even had a 'market' – they were shown before feature films in cinemas. From among directors, Márta Mészáros, Lívia Gyarmathy, Géza Böszörményi, Pál Erdőss and Ferenc Kardos asked him to work on their feature films, but his good relationship remained, for example, with György Szomjas (they worked together on five short films) and also Gábor Bódy, though he could not work with them on full-length feature films later due to clashing timetables. *The Archaic Torso* by Péter Dobai made in the year of *The Press* is noted because a strict critic, László B. Nagy, 'noticed' him in a sharply unbalanced scene. "The camera does not even quiver in the hands of the cameraman, the excellent Lajos Koltai. It follows the sobbing heroine in her frenzy."[6]

The first 'real' film made in the feature film studios was also preceded by a documentary. Lívia Gyarmathy made a successful film with Lajos Koltai under the title *To Whom It may Concern* (1971). The director was daring enough to trust Koltai with her film *Wait a Sec!*, which was a significant film in his career because, following the director's 'Czech like' style, he had to put up a struggle with reality related to full colour, especially in the outdoor scenes. Predictably, the favourite timing of the shots was at sunset or dawn, when the sun still gave a homogenous colouring to the surroundings.

Shooting *Riddance* (1973); first assistant Lajos Fazekas, Márta Mészáros and Lajos Koltai

Koltai was not able to relax for long after that film. He was standing behind the second camera shooting *Petőfi '73* in Pápa when a message came that he should immediately return to Budapest because Márta Mészáros wanted to have a word with him. It turned out that Yvette Bíró, who at the time was still editor-in-chief of *Filmkultúra* and earlier had been assistant for two films by Márta Mészáros, had talked the director into choosing Koltai, who had earlier been able to tune into the specific rhythm of her direction (*In the Lőrinc Spinning-mill*, 1971). Thus he received the script of the film *Riddance* (1973), which aimed to deepen the special feminine angle of Márta Mészáros's previous film, *The Girl* (1967). However, the black and white film was not successful. As Mészáros wrote in her autobiography, she was even tempted by the thought of suicide.[7] Nevertheless, the film, made at the lowest ebb of her career,

[6] B. Nagy, László: *A látvány logikája* (The Logic of Vision). Szépirodalmi Publishers, Budapest, 1974. p. 544
[7] Mészáros, Márta: *Napló magamról* (Diary of Mine). Pelikán Books, Budapest, 1993. p. 59

The first colour film
Wait a Sec!
Géza Böszörményi
on the left,
Lívia Gyarmathy in
the middle with the
cameraman
squatting behind
the camera

has some memorable scenes – the factory atmosphere seemed almost flawless, as did the petty bourgeois environment of a family of first generation professionals. That, of course, also reflected praise for the cameraman.

Thus Lajos Koltai's career was on the rise – but not only his. At the time literature-focused critics were unwilling to regard Hungarian film makers as creative artists. It took the cameramen longest to be accepted, since most of the critics had no idea about the significance of cinematography and thought that a cameraman only had to 'photograph' the actors herded before the lens. It was a rarely acknowledged fact that noted operators were behind the camera.

The situation had begun to change in the second half of the 1950s when due recognition was awarded to cameramen like István Eiben (b.1902), Barna Hegyi (b.1914) and György Illés (b.1914), or Ferenc Szécsényi (b.1922), János Badal (b.1927) and István Hildebrand (b.1928) representing a new generation. In the 1960s another generation appeared, first with János Tóth and Sándor Sára, which was followed by the generation of Elemér Ragályi, József Lőrincz and János Zsombolyai. The first representative of those born in the 1940s, János Kende (*Silence and Cry*, 1968) closely followed them. The boom, as compared to the 1950s, came as a result of improving financial conditions.

Cameramen had to share twenty feature films a year at the time and when Lajos Koltai joined the film studio the sharing did not happen without conflicts, since the Academy was pouring out talented camera operators who naturally wanted to make their first appearance in features. Thus Koltai became a cameraman in a real competitive situation at the beginning of the 1970s. He seems to have been good at 'competing'. Challenges did not pull him back but spurred him to find increasingly bold approaches. In this context he gained his Master's Diploma with the film *At the End of the Road* (1973), directed by Gyula Maár. This black and white film was acknowledged both in Hungary and abroad. Undoubtedly, the film was striking. It was about the twilight of veteran communists and the twilight showed in the pictures. Moreover, the atmosphere and Jozef Króner's outstanding acting made up for the rather uninteresting story. The scene of travelling on a train stands out in the film, practically becoming a film essay, where the semi-darkness, characteristic of the style, lends the characters individual features. The dramatic function of light is perfect – when the disagreeable character enters the compartment he immediately turns on the light, naturally a very dim bulb, and people's openness, which was facilitated by the semi-darkness, is at once transformed into isolation. This little play with the light also points out that a technical effect becomes valuable only if it interprets the situation, which means that a cameraman must analyse the dramatic significance of a situation as much as measure the degree of light.

BETWEEN TRENDS

Openness characterised Lajos Koltai's work in the mid 1970s. He became one of the leading cameramen for documentary features, films which represented the so-called Budapest School, which as a trend enriched public discourse about cinema verite. At the same time, he can also be found shooting art films. The two trends fought with one another, but directors also fought for Lajos Koltai who, as if it were a matter of course, shot at least three films a year. True, at that time he had to make a living not only for himself. In 1969 he married Katalin Bordás, the main character of his film *Improvisations*, and then in quick succession his two daughters, Nóra (1974) and Katalin (1976) were born. Due to his upbringing, if he had family problems he would never air them. His private life has always been taboo to the outside world.

Lajos Koltai did the shooting for *Holiday in Britain* (1974), the best of the Budapest School. Director István Dárday selected the amateur actors exceedingly well. Considering the rather weightless story, they were able to put forward strong arguments to the physically close camera. Their faces expressed their fate and the camera had to explore that, since the dialogue, 'just like in life', did not always make it clear what the character concerned was actually thinking. Koltai was excellent at creating an intimate atmosphere where the characters did not feel they were being watched, even in the family bed, and were able to behave naturally. He achieved this by reducing the technical crew, although he shot the film on colour negative and was careful to match the colours perfectly. It is worth noting how affectionately the camera depicts the village child who is present when the family are discussing whether he can go on holiday to Britain.

Koltai had to return to black and white for the next Dárday film, *The Film Novel* (1975–76). Its length of 273 minutes was unusual and it took two years to shoot. Film stock was in short supply in Hungary and the entire import of colour negative would not have been enough to shoot the story of three sisters over the two years. This film is also a film of faces – the three girls' characters are written on their faces due to the meticulous exploration of the camera. Nevertheless, a long take produced the most popular scene in the film. The well-placed camera shows the family getting up and ready in the morning with so much reality that the viewer tends to believe that Koltai must have made the camera invisible for the actors in order that nothing would disturb them.

Lajos Koltai's farewell to the feature documentary, the less successful *Stratagem* (1979), confirmed for him that the camera operator was the right-hand of not only the director but also the actors. Actors usually try to be nice to cameramen because their on-screen 'beauty' is thought to depend on them. However, it was rather unusual for the film's amateur actor, János Molnár, who played a humiliated president of an agricultural cooperative, to be willing to do the final crying-cum-merrymaking scene only if Lajos Koltai would get blind drunk with him. "Only for you," he would say, and when the camera was taken from Koltai, who never drank much, he also stopped performing. Massaging the nearly unconscious Lajos Koltai's chest around the heart, he said, crying, "Don't leave me here, don't leave me here" and stopped 'acting' for ever. The scene in the film finishes when Koltai stopped shooting.

Why did János Molnár reward him with his friendship? This is quite understandable. Koltai often had to 'make friends' with the actors so that they could cope with the psychological burden the shooting presented.

However, Koltai's professional standing was not elevated particularly high by his feature documentaries, but by some memorable artistic productions. Perhaps that was natural. After all, cameraman Sándor Sára was celebrated alongside Zoltán Huszárik, the director of *Sindbad* (1970), the most significant feature of Hungarian Post-Art-Nouveau. Similarly, cameraman János Tóth's role was emphasised among the makers of the internationally acknowledged film *Love* (1970), directed by Károly Makk.

Katalin Bordás, the "star" of *Improvisations* (1965)

An evening of the long engagement

Two films of the artistic genre brought acknowledgement to Lajos Koltai: *Mrs Déry, Where are You?* (1975) by Gyula Maár, and *On the Side-Line* (1976) by Péter Szász. With Maár's film, the historic environment and period costumes, in addition to the actors' theatre experience, are important elements. However, it is not the rather artificial agelessness of the film which attracts the viewer of today but the 'eternal' psychological conflict of an artist's existence. What is better? To grasp the first call of petty bourgeois security or watch helplessly as former greatness dissolves as a result of biological aging?

The role of the legendary actress, Mrs Déry, was played by Mari Törőcsik. She was surrounded by renowned actors of the Hungarian theatre, including Ferenc Kállai, Tamás Major, Mária Sulyok, Imre Ráday and Kornél Gelley. Even the role of the boy playing the piano was played by none other than the pianist András Schiff.

The family: Katalin, Lajos and their two daughters, Nóra (b. 1974) and Katalin (b. 1976)

The high-level theatre culture created the atmosphere of the shooting for Lajos Koltai. He understood that cinematography here had to emphasise art and he succeeded with patience and almost painful precision, but also with much daring in that the colour negative would be as underexposed as in his black and white films, which were regarded as experimental. The pictorial unity of the film was provided by a basic tone composed for ten-minute sequences. The atmosphere was determined by the colourless, dark patches of parts left in shade and semi-darkness, suggesting a thorough study of Rembrandt's portraits. This literally translated the central idea of the film into images – the melancholy of aging and disappearance.

Most viewers were affected by the film. Indeed, the makers themselves, after viewing the rushes, could not help dancing euphorically on the steps of the Kecskemét theatre, which had served as the location of the film. They thought they had found gold. Yet there were some who were not so happy, such as the director of the Hungarian Film Export-Import Company, who thought the film would be unsellable due to the techniques applied. It turned out not to be so – Lajos Koltai received the first *personal* acknowledgement of his career (from the Hungarian film critics) and Mari Törőcsik was awarded with the Prize for Best Actress at Cannes.

Melancholy is also the key to *On the Side-Line*. "The 'concurrence' of finite and infinite cannot be reached by any theory and can be interpreted only

A typical shot from *Mrs Déry, Where are you?*
(Gyöngyvér Vígh, Ferenc Kállai, Mária Sulyok and Mari Törőcsik)

allegorically at best," writes László Földényi in his book on melancholy.[8]
The great thing about the film by Péter Szász is that we feel he has managed to conjure such concurrence naturally and allegorically for the viewer, even for moments (in a longer scene). The main character (Ferenc Kállai) would like to be committed to something, but the experience escapes him, even in his love of

football, which in his case is rather psychotic. Koltai realised that the pictures had to float on the borderline of the real and the unreal. The hero's image should be both real and abstract. He succeeded in doing that in a less lively scene when the main character only talks in an emotional way – he is telling his life story as a matter of course, as if after a satisfying Sunday dinner. We can almost feel the passing of time. We have fallen into the cameraman's trap. It becomes dark during Kállai's monologue; the lighting effect is part of the unity which is

The "Koltai style" is being formed; Péter Szász might as well play in the film *On the Side-Line* (1976)

dictated by the rhythm of the text and the camera movement. This scene presents us with a real experience. Infinite values glitter for a moment in the finite life. The miracle has happened, for which it is worth torturing actors, the crew and especially yourself with repeat shots.

We should also note that Koltai took the football match at the centre of the story to his 'home' field. He persuaded the director to create the 'stadium' of a small town on the field of the Old Buda Brickyard. The field was special because it almost leans on to a hill; thus if the camera is at the usual eye-height it does not show the sky above the characters' heads, but a pastel-coloured mass of greenery.

In those years Lajos Koltai realised that it was not the highest degree of his craft to force his own style on a film, but, if he could, to express the 'style of things' in pictures. In order to do this he had to abandon the small 'cheat' directors of feature documentaries employed in the interest of showing reality, namely looking for the

[8] Földényi F., László: *Melankólia* (Melancholy). Second, revised edition, Akadémiai Publishing House, Budapest, 1992. p. 98

faded and threadbare in everything so that they would make us see the beauty in the wrinkles and folds of objects and people. They were scared of spectacles traditionally thought to be beautiful, as if they represented evil. To be haggard and hard seemed naturally alright, at least to the extent that it showed something real. That intention made the film *Adoption* (1975), directed by Márta Mészáros, memorable. It made her suddenly famous by winning the 'Golden Bear' in Berlin and the Gold Plaque in Chicago. No doubt, the cameraman's work also contributed to the prizes, although Hungarian reviews looked for a fly in the ointment. For example, they criticised the film for being monochrome.

The 'style of things' defined the cinematographic excellence in Ferenc András's first film, *Rain and Shine* (1976). The daring attempt to shoot a film with professional actors in the style of a documentary was successful. The cameraman's role in the film was, of necessity, recognised as being more than a service element. Lajos Koltai even had to perform the assistant's tasks in the central scene of the film, the 'blow out', in order to avoid the lights and movement being contradictory in the takes, which took ten days to complete. It was then that he experienced one of the most difficult tasks of filming, namely when a scene revolves around a series of closely-knit shots. In this case, the food and the hands holding out for it, the characters' eyes looking at one another and the chaotic talking created a real symphony. Koltai had the 'musical notes' in his pocket. He prepared an awfully long list of shots, which had to be strictly followed as the filming was done. Finally, he treated light in an unusual way, compared to his earlier work. He lit in exterior; the light was pouring in from the side of the covered porch, reproducing midday hours throughout. The successful film, awarded the main prize at Karlovy Vary, involved personal recognition for the cameraman, too. Of course, Koltai appreciated it, but he had no time to ponder on the success. He also had to experience what it was like when a film failed.

In the event, there were a few such films in the 1970s. The weak script of the young director Lajos Fazekas could not be filled with life (*On the Run*, 1974). The second film by Géza Böszörményi, *The Car* (1974), was not popular either,

Above the city: Lajos Koltai, the cameraman of *The American Cigarette* (1977)

although it was a hard film to shoot since a lot of daring car rides had to be produced.

Pál Gábor's historical film *Epidemic* (1975), which started with a great impetus but wound down completely by the end, only received a Grand Prix in Cairo. However, Koltai was able to show that he was highly skilled not only at lighting interiors but also at depicting natural environments. However, his following two films with Gyula Maár were not successful, although the film *Flare and Flicker* is an ambitious piece of work, a sort of catalogue of styles. Besides being a 'reward performance' for Mari Törőcsik, who achieved international fame in the role of Mrs Déry, the camera created a true night club atmosphere and synthesised it into an experience of fate in the scene of a minor character, that of Lenke Lorán, otherwise a comedy actress. The adaptation for television of Mór Jókai's novel, *The Woman of Lőcse in White* (1976), again with Mari Törőcsik in the leading role, was a noteworthy experiment in romantic style. However, the film, shot on 16mm colour, did not adapt to the visual requirements of the magic box (colour television was still rare in Hungary at the time) and the spectacle 'remained in the camera', to twist a common saying.

The film *American Cigarette* (1977), adapting a radio play by István Csurka, who became noted as an extreme right politician some two decades later, had little success but provided much experience. Although the director, János Dömölky, involved two great personalities of Hungarian theatre, Hilda Gobbi and Zoltán Makláry, for the role of two elderly street sweepers, Lajos Koltai

with the camera was able to witness that a poor literary screenplay remained hidebound despite the acting of two geniuses. But even such a film has its later use. Dömölky allowed much freedom for his cameraman, who in the pub scene was able naturally and instinctively to prepare for other noted pub scenes, for example in Péter Gothár's films.

WITHOUT TRENDS

The time came when there was no need to be supported by the thrust of trends and schools. At the end of the 1970s Lajos Koltai was the cameraman for several films which made their mark in world cinema. The first such film was undoubtedly *Angi Vera* (1978), in which ripened the non-too-easy cooperation with Pál Gábor. Gábor, who, in addition to directing, was a professor at the Academy of Drama and Film alongside one of the most respected masters in cinematography, Zoltán

Vera Pap and Tamás Dunai (*Angi Vera*, 1978)

Fábri, realised that Koltai, a generation younger than himself, was also competent at defining the pictorial image.

Angi Vera was not alone in its theme. At the end of the 1970s Hungarian film makers, employing a shrewd tactical approach, were allowed to depict the 'cult of personality', a dark period of Hungarian history. Pál Gábor and the studio where he made the film realised that the way to tell the truth was to reflect the period in human relations. Lajos Koltai's virtues in documentaries were utilised in creating an informal atmosphere, and at the same time both he and the director 'freed' colour and light from supporting a realist environment. He boldly faded the colours. Thus, for example, he only used a single bulb in the emotionally important love scene, being of the opinion that lighting the takes from different sources would have been empty decoration. So the colours cut up the picture into several colour islands but provided a united basic tone, which radiated throughout the entire film. The viewers did not have to put their criticism about the film into words, they felt instinctively that it was *cold*. That was also underlined by the snowy scenery at the end, a favourite motif of Koltai, which, despite picture post card connotations, suggests the fundamental idea of the film with its dirty grey patches reaching under the horizon and its shivering cold.

Cecília Esztergályos
and Pál Hetényi
(*A Priceless Day,* 1979)

After *Angi Vera*, it was natural for András Kovács to choose Koltai as cameraman for *The Stud Farm* (1978). Cooperation did not seem easy with the didactic director who was thinking in terms of dialogue even to the detriment of images. However, Koltai was attracted by a new opportunity of depicting the 1950s and the work involved much interesting and challenging exterior shooting, since the story took place at a stud farm near the southern border of Hungary. The difficulties increased during shooting. Since the scenes were not shot in chronological order, the 'real lighting' changed from strong sunshine to misty and foggy semi-darkness and a united basic tone had to be mixed from the natural variety by adding artificial lights.

Film critics were surprised to see that András Kovács had made a "film-like film",[9] which unfortunately was not able to enjoy the international career it deserved. The Hungarian cultural authorities had it withdrawn from the competing

[9] Gantner, Ilona: *Népszava*, (daily) 12 October 1978

János Derzsi, Pál Hetényi, Cecília Esztergályos
and two 'real' characters in the dinner scene of
A Priceless Day (1979)

The most valued items in Lajos Koltai's collection are the crew photographs made on the last day of shooting a film. Pictured here is the team which created *A Priceless Day* (1979)

films at the Berlin Festival, because the festival's director would not bow to the Soviet demand to remove Michael Cimino's *The Deer Hunter* from the programme. In Locarno, where there was no such conflict of a political nature, Lajos Koltai received the respected Ernest Artaria Prize for camera work. Yet he did not have similar success with the next Márta Mészáros film, which had Jan Nowiczki in the leading role. Hungarian film critics did not relate favourably to the films directed by Mészáros and the displeasure was increased by the fact that her standing abroad steadily grew.

Just like at Home (1978) was an important film in Koltai's career. A gifted child actress, Zsuzsa Czinkóczi, played a main character. Although she did not have to be 'discovered', it had happened in the film *No Man's Daughter* (1975) by László Ranódy, but to instruct her with love before the camera presented a task proving to be profitable in the future (the word instruct here is not used as a synonym for a director's instructions).

In the end the convergence of fortunate accidents showed clearly at the turn of the 1970s and 1980s in that Lajos Koltai definitively became one of the top Hungarian cameramen. Péter Gothár's film *A Priceless Day* was shown on 6 December 1979 and the film *Confidence*, directed by István Szabó, followed on 10 January 1980.

A Priceless Day was actually somewhat of a shot in the dark for Lajos Koltai. The director wanted one thing – everything to be different from before. That cheered the cameraman, who did not want to have standard tasks but to experiment. The lighting had to be suitable for several things to happen during a take; the cameraman had to take the camera in hand and have an eye for what was actually most important in terms of the story. Thus Koltai held the camera, which was not new for him, and with a wide-angle lens he went as near the actors as he could, while at the same time they noticed him as little as a speck of dust in a light ray. That special situation developed whereby, as is said in film theory, the camera 'penetrated reality', not as a scalpel but as an almost chance element of the natural environment. The effect was shocking. Processes were not interrupted by cuts (should an editing shot be applied in order to clear up something, both the director and the cameraman regarded it as defeat). The end of the film represented the peak performance of the experiment. The two actresses, Cecília Esztergályos and Judit Pogány, the latter enjoying with great success her first leading role in a film, played the scene in a railway restaurant car, which Koltai solved with a narrowing round movement of the camera. His spiral movement emphasised the two actresses among uninteresting people in an uninteresting space and created the necessary island experience which the viewer knew and often wished he had. It is the only psychological space where a person can talk about himself honestly. *A Priceless Day* was praised by Hungarian film critics and, moreover, was awarded the 'Leone d'oro' prize for first film in Venice.

When preparing for *Confidence* István Szabó had a film in mind which no longer depicted the 1950s but the moment when the total distrust characteristic of the era was born. He wanted a cameraman to suit this idea. He found the ideal partner in Lajos Koltai. The most frequently appearing scenery in the film was constructed in a studio. However, the walls could not be altered so that everything would seem real in spatial movements. Light became of outstanding significance in this enclosed interior. The director and the cameraman 'mixed' the light based on shades of green, allowing the inclusion of both reality and dream in the same quality. Since the story had a solid dramatic line and the leading players, Ildikó Bánsági and Péter Andorai, gave their top performance, Lajos Koltai had the opportunity to try out visual effects which related only to a given take and did not have to be included throughout the film.

The beginning of a long and successful artistic relationship – István Szabó, Ildikó Bánsági and Lajos Koltai while shooting *Confidence* (1979)

Ildikó Bánsági and
Péter Andorai
(*Confidence*, 1979)

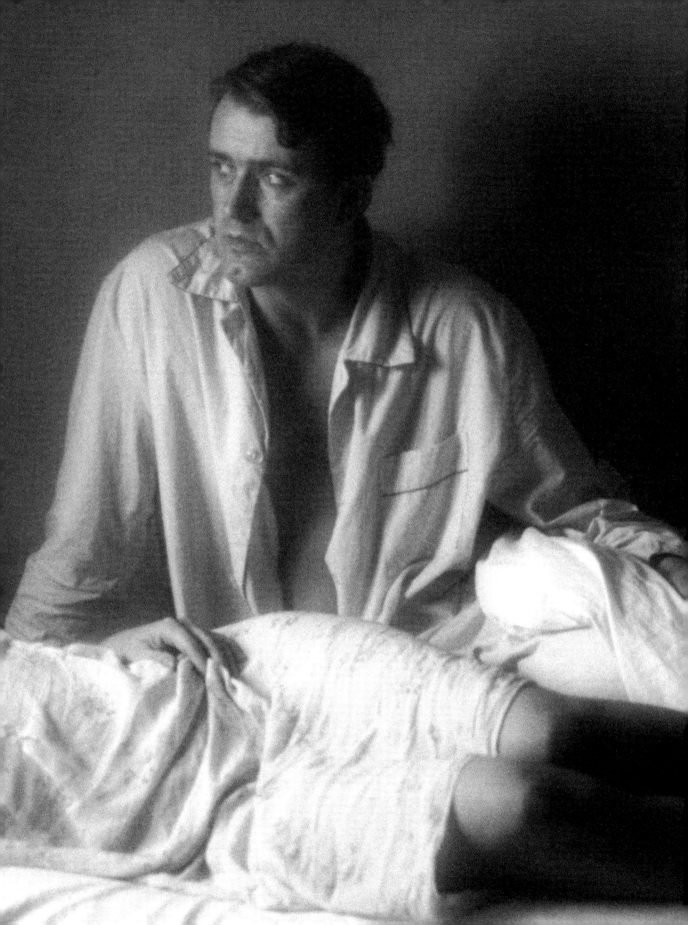

The real green colour of a lampshade or the red of a flashing flame did not fit the basic tone, but the viewer, not taking them in consciously, was encouraged to seek interconnections and finally was allowed to suppose the existence of an abstract light. It characterised the historical situation intimately when rats in human form emerged from sewage pipes.

LESSONS OF HISTORY

Without doubt István Szabó had an effect on Koltai. His precision, clarity of instructions, the objective nature of his ideas and his critical approach represented a model which could be followed. Koltai often remembered the interpreting instructions as a kind of "Szabó school".[10] It was really an experience to hear that Szabó not only analysed the visible matters but also what was beyond, namely what the history of Central Europe meant in this area. The three films which journalists superficially called the 'trilogy' (the reason being that Klaus Maria Brandauer, who became an international star, was the leading

With director István Szabó and leading actor Péter Andorai of *The Green Bird* (1979) in front of the Berlin office of producer Manfred Durniok

actor in all three) represented time travel for Lajos Koltai, since those films depicted a period which he had not experienced due to his age. He learnt that something *indirect* can be the source of experience as something *direct*: the personality does not disappear when the fathers' and grandfathers' story has to be retold in order to make larger contexts understood. *Mephisto* (81), *Colonel Redl* (1984) and *Hanussen* (88) differed from Koltai's former films in respect to their production. All three could be made only in international co-production, although foreign partners acknowledged in all three cases that the Hungarian producer was the ringmaster.

After making *Confidence* István Szabó and Lajos Koltai made a German television film, which was later overshadowed by the three films. However, in the film the producer was able to try out whether the two met international standards from a production point of view. As can be seen, they did, and this TV film has a greater significance with respect to *Fateless* than has previously been considered. The film *Der grüne Vogel* (*The Green Bird*) took Lajos Koltai in 1979 to the locations which would provide the environment for *Fateless*. Naturally, it is not the location which is essential but the central theme of *The Green Bird*.

[10] Csala, Károly–Fazekas, Eszter: *A fény festője. Koltai Lajos operatőr* (Painter of Light, Lajos Koltai, the Cameraman). Osiris, Budapest, 2001. p. 86

István Znamenák and Lajos Őze (*Time Stands Still*, 1981)

Lajos Koltai
and István Szabó
looking for
the best angle
and picture cut;
Mephisto (1981)

Meditation
in the water
– a search
for ideal lights

FACING PAGE:
Klaus Maria
Brandauer's
Mephisto mask

OVERLEAF:
The final
sequence of
Mephisto (1981)

The film presents a confrontation with Auschwitz, which seemed to be 'unessential' beside the question of 'who defeats whom' in the period of the Cold War. Therapist-director István Szabó strongly suggested that the Holocaust had not yet been dealt with by society. Thus Lajos Koltai faced a theme which the camera could not deal with only as a technical matter. Nevertheless, the camera could not shake in his hands either through indignation or due to being overwhelmed, and his objective perspective could not cloud. It became clear for Koltai that Auschwitz was not actually a 'Jewish matter'.

It concerns *us* in the broadest sense of the word, 'the silent majority', before whose indifferent or fright-stricken eyes the genocide of the 20th century planned with engineering precision took place.

Success for *Colonel Redl* (1984) – István Szabó, Klaus Maria Brandauer, Lajos Koltai and Károly Eperjes

To put it briefly, *The Green Bird* is the most important link in the chain which leads to *Fateless*.

The films *Mephisto*, *Colonel Redl* and *Hanussen* modified Lajos Koltai's idea concerning pictorial unity. Since each film spans longer periods of time and takes place in varied locations, it would have been impossible to put each into one type of basic tone. But before the shooting had started he and Szabó discussed and decided on the basic colours. Thus, for example, *Mephisto* is characterised by shades of gold and purple, while field grey is given to *Colonel Redl*. Actions and episodes belonging together have their base tone, which gave an opportunity for Koltai to use magical variations. He could produce the intensive shades of the theatre world and enjoy the impressionism of airy colourful exteriors. Since his director was absolutely at home in the subject, he could also mobilise his education in fine arts before an 'appreciative audience'. Some of the compositions, especially in *Hanussen*, corresponded to the fantastic world of Otto Dix and George Grosz. The feeling of chaos was also promoted by the source of light being rather down and not above as it is considered 'natural'. An observant viewer could also notice the important role architecture had in these films. They suggest that power wants to express itself in buildings. It is enough for us to see a barracks interior or a panelled study and we immediately know at what stage the story is and what we can expect. Invention permeates even the compulsorily spectacular scenes, such as a ball room swirl. If we compare the two balls in *Mephisto* and *Colonel Redl* we must realise there is no scene for its own sake. One characterises the General, the other the Heir, that is what the function of the scenes is, which is far from the usual sweet feel of a ball scene.

These films certainly stand out from the average of Hungarian film production

This striking picture arose from something entirely practical; Lajos Koltai is setting the lighting during the shooting of *Hanussen*

Lajos Koltai with István Szabó at the time of *Hanussen* (1988)

and thus, as things go, the film makers received not only benevolent recognition. The reviewers most often criticised them for lacking a 'Hungarian character' or a poetic 'personal attitude', which they never expanded on. Furthermore, they told a story which was not 'popular' in Hungarian cinematography at the beginning of the 1980s.[11] Even well-meaning critics said that by making the story central, István Szabó and Lajos Koltai had moved dangerously close to American films. The Oscar for *Mephisto* counted as the pure evidence.

In the beginning Lajos Koltai could prevent himself from being fired at by being the cameraman for Péter Gothár's outstandingly significant film *Time Stands Still* (1981), which received all existing awards in Hungary a year after *Mephisto*, and which was also noticed abroad (for example, with the Prize of Youth in Cannes). Koltai only had to be more radical for the sake of the film than he had been with *A Priceless Day*.

The camera moved even nearer to the actors and it was worth it, since we can observe the face of one of the greatest Hungarian actors, Lajos Őze, furrowed by history in absolutely close shots in a pub. The face of the actor is giving a lesson on Central European survival – even "shit is shitted on", he says, expressing the feeling of many – to the 16-year-old István

The child Redl
(*Colonel Redl*, 1984)

Znamenák. (After his role in the film Znamenák decided to become an actor, as did Sándor Sőth of the same age, who in the end became a director.) Nevertheless, special lighting was also required for the face, which produced a daring idea. Koltai placed neon lights under the counter. And, as an unusual gesture, from the camera he constantly shouted: "Heads nearer to each other!" The fact, that certain layers of the Kodak negative had been made sensitive 'spoiling' perfect colours and also

[11] "A return to the pattern and recipes of film making (plot, effect, spectacle and acting) which have been effective in the past decade and 'reinvented' by Hollywood recently. It fits in the process which has reinstated the story and spectacle recently, ensuring entertainment and professionalism as priority against spare, often immature form and unkempt thought." Gervai, András: Redl ezredes (Colonel Redl). *Film, Színház, Muzsika*, 16 February 1985. p. 4

László Gálffi and Klaus Maria Brandauer
(*Colonel Redl*, 1984)

Duel at dawn
(*Colonel Redl*,
1984)

Klaus Maria Brandauer,
Ildikó Bánsági,
Erland Josephson and
Adrianna Biedrzyńska
in a famous Budapest
coffee house
(*Hanussen*, 1988)

that a technician's home made-device sprinkled chalk dust in the air, contributed to the special, 'floating' atmosphere, resulting in something more like a painting than a photograph.

One consequence of the special effects was that Koltai, stuck behind the camera, became ill with fever. The illness, however, could also have been psychosomatic. A difficult person, Péter Gothár was able to quarrel badly even with his cameraman, generally regarded as quite easy-going. Shooting had to be suspended and then everything continued as if nothing had happened between the two people in charge. Nevertheless, it may hardly be an accident that since then they have never again found a free period of time in which to work together.

The efforts proved to be good investment. In 1983 Koltai was invited to Los Angeles for a screening of *Time Stands Still*. In the city of films Dezső Magyar took his former cameraman, still struggling with English, under his wing.

At the end of the film there was absolute silence. Koltai thought it had flopped, but he was soon told that silence was the greatest recognition. At last the much experienced American profession had seen a film which shocked and magnetised them. They saw something new and likable. The cinematography of *Time Stands Still* became a standard to such an extent that a cunning Hungarian cameraman pretended to be Koltai in Hollywood and the name opened the door to his career – until the real Lajos Koltai appeared on the scene and his face, in addition to his films, became well-known in the profession.

MANDOKI, BRANDAUER AND OTHERS

Lajos Koltai could have rested on his laurels in the 1980s. Instead, he unexpectedly got into adventures without promising immediate success, either at home or abroad. He tried to insist on only one person, István Szabó, and the feeling was mutual. Szabó made films in the following two decades only with him.

Let us note Koltai's Hungarian films first. He worked with directors Lajos Fazekas and János Dömölky again – in vain. Neither *Not Yet the Day* (1980) nor *Roofs at Dawn* (1986) enhanced the story of Hungarian cinema (though Koltai did receive professional recognition for the latter in Hungary). While he was still shooting the most successful film of the Budapest School (*The Princess* by Pál Erdőss in 1983 was awarded the Gold Camera prize at Cannes), he was preparing with great expectations for the films *Guernica* (1982) by Ferenc Kósa and *Heavenly Hosts* (1983) by Ferenc Kardos. He had to be disappointed in both instances. He had to realise that ideological film making, where images as compared to the text containing the references to literary references have only an accompanying role, was not his cup of tea. Yet the opposite did not satisfy him either. Kardos, analysing the situation precisely, was made depressed during shooting by his own mistakes in relation to casting, and put himself in his cameraman's hands, saying he could try out whatever he wanted in the film. The essence of the problem was that

Lajos Koltai
did not remain
behind the camera;
pictured here
helping an actress
during a take of
Not Yet the Day
(1980)

the censors had allowed the filming of a parable written years before. Meanwhile the script 'cooled off', and even the radical upgrading achieved by Koltai and his camera did not help.

In those years the question, of course, was not whether Lajos Koltai would become a cameraman but when he would be a world famous director of photography.

International fame in the profession demands two things: the world of film criticism and film history takes up your name and you are known to the necessary degree in the citadel of the film industry, America. Both ways to world fame require resolute will, confidence, love of adventure and a lucky character, and of course circumstances also help. Accept that you are European in America and in Europe insist on being Hungarian.

You can decide whether it was resolute will or fortune which played a bigger role in making *Angi Vera*. That film proved to be an important step on the way to world fame. The story goes that a telex arrived at Hungarofilm, the then film import-export company, with the request from a director called Luis Mandoki saying that he would like to ask the cameraman of *Angi Vera* to shoot his film, work on which was beginning immediately. He did not even know Koltai's name, only that he needed *that* Hungarian cameraman. Such requests cannot be resisted and so Koltai found himself being expected to create a match for *Angi Vera* in the images of the film *Gaby – A True Story* (1986), which takes us to the world of motor-disordered people living in wheelchairs with admiringly beautiful emotions. The renowned actresses, Liv Ullmann, whom Koltai had only admired in Bergman's films, alongside Norma Aleandro and Rachel Chagall, made the task memorable. The film attracted as much attention as was needed for the big Hollywood studios to take notice of the director and the director of photography. Yet those who might think that one battle is enough to take in the LA 'film fortress', with its union protection and other restrictions, will soon wake up to the cruel reality – one proof is not final evidence.

Nevertheless Koltai was not without work in America. Andrei Konchalovsky commissioned him for his *Homer and Eddie* (1989). It was an attractive offer since the performers included Whoopi Goldberg and James Belushi, and in this typical road movie Koltai could make his vision of America collide with reality. Needless to say that he, like most central Europeans, had a familiar picture of America, the melting pot, the outlines of which were made up by messages sent home by millions who, in the words of the poet Attila József, "stumbled out".

The sun shines strongly throughout the film but there is no warmth, only endless roads, and the man from a small European country feels he will never get to the end of the road. The shooting itself took them from Los Angeles through the Nevada desert and all the way to the icy north, each day at a different location.

The first personal recognition – film critics' prize (1974)

Koltai sometimes thought he was pursuing a hopeless struggle for the small joy one must feel after a successful take. He often recalled György Illés, whose main idea in his teaching at the Academy was that film was a joy and if you did not have any joy then there was big trouble. Before you carried on you must try to see why the enjoyment had gone. Konchalovskiy also struggled with the material but at least for him the film brought some satisfaction by winning the main prize, the Gold Shell in San Sebastian, that is to say in Europe.

Good old Europe waited for Lajos Koltai to come back in the person of Klaus Maria Brandauer. The actor took it in his head that he not only wanted to perform but also direct. Of course, he knew himself that he could do both only if he had a reliable person by the camera who could respond to every question adequately. It was impossible to resist Brandauer's beseeching and anyway Koltai never put requests in a theoretical order. The theme of the film was also interesting. *Georg Elser* (1989) is about the man who placed an explosive device in the Bürgerbräukeller in Munich where Hitler gave a speech to his followers on 8 November 1939.

The story of the attempt on Hitler's life cannot but be told in a vivid way. Elser was caught an hour before the attack, attempting to cross the Swiss border without the necessary papers but with objects in his pocket connected to the attack. It is also debated whether he was a perfect plotter and Hitler was saved by finishing his speech early and leaving the cellar or he was an extremely naive person who was used by those competing for power in the Nazi leadership. But for posterity he could be the 'silent German' who dared to act at a time of unrestrained terror, showing that frenzied ideas did not infect all the people. The film was naturally successful due to its many German references, among others Brandauer was awarded for the role of Elser at the Berlin Film Festival.

Rarely seen together: László Kovács (*Easy Rider*, 1969), György Illés, Vilmos Zsigmond (*Sugarland Express*, 1974) and Lajos Koltai

The beauty of directing – and what precedes it, all the difficulty of bringing a film together – had tempted Lajos Koltai, too. I remember that in 1985 Iván Markó, the former dancer at the Béjart Ballet, would have liked a feature film to be made about the Győr Ballet, which Markó himself had run and made famous. He wanted Koltai to be both director and cameraman. In another plan, Koltai and I once called on the author Endre Fejes concerning an even more concrete proposal. Fejes was going to write a screenplay "exclusively for Sutyi" about a district of Budapest, the sweet Józsefváros, where his lyrical stories were set. That was a great honour, since the writer certainly disliked the television films based on his works.

The plans were blown away by the break-up of the Hungarian film industry at the end of the decade. The Hungarian Film Production Company went bankrupt and was then liquidated. The expert workforce was dismissed. This meant that a professional culture stretching back half a century was crippled. In short, Hungarian film, which had been in the vanguard of the political struggles behind the 1989-90 changes, had the ground cut from under its very feet.

THE 1990s

It was understandable that many in the profession looked abroad to enhance their career. Lajos Koltai was one who succeeded in this. He reaped the harvest of the 1980s in the 1990s. He only shot a Hungarian film when István Szabó brought the productions of his films to Hungary out of a sense of duty – assuming he could persuade his producers.

Koltai's American list is rather extensive and it is noteworthy that the big studios worked with him. *Descending Angel* (1990) was directed by Jeremy Kagan and financed by HBO, which produced *Perfect Witness* (1990), directed by Robert Mandel. Universal, meanwhile, produced Luis Mandoki's best film, *White Palace* (1990). The artistic gangster film *Mobsters*, directed by Michael Karbelnikoff, was also a Universal production. Similarly, studios at the top of the American film industry produced two further films by Mandoki (*Born Yesterday* 1993, *When a Man loves a Woman*, 1994). Warner Brothers financed *Wrestling Ernest Hemingway* (1993), directed by Randa Haines, and Arne Glimcher's *Just Cause* (1995). Koltai also worked for Paramount – he was the cameraman for *Home for the Holidays* (1995), directed by Jodie Foster, and he also made *Mother* (1996) there. Albert Brooks directed the latter and he also played the leading role. Finally, so as not leave XXth Century Fox out of the list, the old studio produced Martha Coolidge's *Out to Sea* (1997). This was the film, which in Hungarian translation had the title *To Sea, Ol' Man*, gained him the recognition of the stars of American

Lajos Koltai during the shooting of *Mother* (1996). The director, Albert Brooks (on the right) listens attentively to his cameraman's proposals

Characterised by self-confidence...

and giving a helping hand at any time

With Glenn Close
during the shooting
of *Meeting Venus*
(1991)

comedy, Jack Lemmon and Walter Matthau, which in its value cannot be expressed by any prize.

These American productions add up to eleven films. Have they anything in common? Considering genre they do not, since they include social drama, melodrama and comedy. Undoubtedly they share a common feature in as much as Lajos Koltai wanted to meet the requirement which they commissioned him for – to be different from others. Conflicts were generated because the studios wanted the difference to be within calculable limits, namely not to be radical. The task was to make the producer, director and actors happy.

While shooting his American films Koltai had to struggle with the philosophy which says that *funny* is good, and if something is not funny it cannot be good. He could not help noticing that infantilism exuberating from American films is not an artificial formation, society also mostly observes itself in an infantile way. Those who do not follow the order of 'keep smiling' are not funny. In the event, a conflict between Koltai and Meg Ryan was not funny. She had to get drunk from a bottle of vodka for her role in *When a Man Loves a Woman*, but she wanted be fit the following day so that her funny image created in the viewers would not be doubted for a single moment. The particular disagreement went as far as involving Lajos Koltai, who was generally noted for never making a scandal during shooting, moreover he rather smoothed things over.
This time he kicked out the actress's make-up artist, who was acting as an informer, spying on him. One had to learn that something like that happened in America.

In the company
of Hollywood legends
Jack Lemmon
and Walter Matthau
(*Out to Sea*, 1997)

Lajos Koltai's mark does not show in all the films. His personal style can be seen mostly in the films where he was able to have a say dramaturgically. It was important for him to have his own sense of justice accepted and put in. *White Palace*, directed by Luis Mandoki, was such a film, where as an exceptional appraisal, Susan Sarandon said: "I trust you absolutely forever." That was not empty talk. She would allow close-ups only if Lajos Koltai himself was behind the camera, and not his assistant. "I want to see you and nobody else," she said. Let us not think that this was an overheated manner of a star. The actress felt safe when the direction of her look moved away from the axis a little and she saw Lajos Koltai, since she felt the empathy for her, whereas others only observed indifferently what she was doing for her money.

The peculiarities of American filming often thrilled Koltai, but the work still did not satisfy him. He felt the ebb when, during an informal dinner in Los Angeles given by Vilmos Zsigmond for cameramen, Vittorio Storaro remarked that he had just seen the film *Born Yesterday*. "You know," he said, "anybody could have filmed it…. By the way it was very nice…" Later Koltai himself would re-tell the story, which after all shows that he is aware of judgement even when his own work is criticised. Storaro's remark deeply saddened him and film making suddenly became meaningless for him. He thought he had sacrificed his personality on the altar of the studios' demands. Depression, however, did not last long. Another commission came. Randa Haines sent him the script for *Wrestling Ernest Hemingway*, which immediately got his fantasy working over the images. The film, which takes place among the elderly in Florida, seemed quite European in its approach to people, and the feeling was enhanced by the three outstanding actors, Richard Harris, Robert Duvall and Shirley MacLaine. Self-irony glitters in their playing together, which was harsh but lovable, and not wryly funny in any way. The three great actors let the camera near their faces. They accepted their wrinkles and crinkles and in return Lajos Koltai showed with the force of pictures that there was beauty in age if it was coupled with wisdom and human warmth. The cameraman trusted the faces and this trust tamed even a wild beast like Robert Duvall, who regarded directors in general as well as in this case as a negligible part of a film. When Koltai was composing the lighting for one of his scenes, Duvall simply sent the stand-in away. Indeed, to shine the light on the actor was a great experience. One finds the best possible solution and the actors honour it with their love.

Among colleagues in Hollywood (left to right: Douglas Milsome, Vittorio Storaro, Lajos Koltai, Vilmos Zsigmond and George Spiro Dibie)

Despite the difficulties, Lajos Koltai did not for a moment regard his American films made in the 1990s as futile. They contained plenty of lessons. First of all he learnt to speak the language of American actors, stars and important supporting characters who were carrying the plot on their backs. He learnt it concretely and also in abstract. That was not easy. He had conflicts even with such a great actor as Sean Connery whose biggest worry in *Just Cause* concerned when the shooting was going to finish. He was in a hurry since he wanted to go on holiday. He drove the crew and naturally the 'clever' ones blamed the Hungarian director of photography for the delays, saying he was too slow with lighting. Of course, that was not true since it was actually Koltai who saved one and a half days from the first four days of shooting. Yet in spite of that he knew that if the star had something against the cameraman the latter had had it. Indeed, Vilmos Zsigmond had already been contacted to take over the film and 'create order'. Zsigmond naturally did not agree to the task of a butcher. In the end Koltai asked Connery what the trouble was with him. Nothing. Only slowness. Koltai showed that the opposite was true. He was the best prepared for each shooting day. Making peace took place when the rushes were viewed. Connery understood that the thriller would be a bit different from the others. The pictures not only met the sacred requirement of television visibility in America but had also captured the atmosphere which derived from the character of the interiors and exteriors in Florida. The atmosphere in the film is not only a necessary background but also the tangible psychological space in the story. To Connery's credit, he honoured Koltai's efforts and surprised him with a personal gift, a rare honour – a bottle of champagne and his photograph dedicated to "my dear Lajos". In any case, in this film "dear Lajos" struggled back from a hollow depth to the level of this recognition. However, this is not rare in America. Whoever is down if he has enough perseverance and talent can still be up. Only 'silly Europeans', who have given up being self-confident, would collapse after some disappointment by not coping with a blow to their great self-esteem.

CONFIDENT GREATNESS

The István Szabó and Lajos Koltai cooperation continued in the 1990s. Most striking is that in this period both experimented with genres, and with different photographic and dramaturgical approaches. They did not remain at the point of copying their achieved results, which is significant since to remain the same as your image is a requirement in America.

In 1990 they made the film *Meeting Venus* with David Puttnam's inspiring cooperation as producer. It is an effective and optimistic simile of Europe, whereby origin, language and the past do not matter, except in terms of what you can add to the culture which is the main token of European identity. István Szabó also underlined this idea by, for example, having the Hungarian conductor played by a Danish actor in the opera company preparing for *Tannhäuser*, and an American star, Glenn Close, play the role of a German soprano. The genre, comedy (previously absent from Szabó's oeuvre), provided the opportunity for a freer treatment of the material. Although Lajos Koltai had made comedies, it was he who said that it was one of the most difficult tasks. This is undoubtedly true, since it is not each participant who has to be funny in a European comedy, rather the atmosphere has to be both cheerful and capable of sustaining dramatic elements, as can be seen in Shakespeare's comedies, which serve as the European reference.

Enikő Börcsök and Johanna ter Steege (*Sweet Emma, Dear Boebe*, 1991)

If we regard *Meeting Venus* as a composition for a large orchestra, the master-piece made in the following year, *Sweet Emma, Dear Boebe*, can be called a chamber piece, since it is based on the captivating duality of two outstanding actresses, Johanna ter Steege and Enikő Börcsök. It is more than a decade since the first screening of the film (20 March 1992), but that time has shown that this film by Szabó and Koltai, which in an exemplary manner they made from a modest budget, is the only one which was able to encapsulate the Hungarian systemic change from the aspect of human values. Szabó thought it right to have the subtitle of 'sketches', which was also meant for Koltai. There was no artificial basic atmosphere in the film and he could freely give differing characters to the scenes. Moreover, he could make the most of his skills gained in documentaries. In the event, the film found itself in the centre of cross-fire. Some Hungarian professionals criticised Szabó for not utilising the budget he was entitled to, since it set a bad precedent, and film critics were willing to acknowledge only Johanna ter Steege's acting. Nevertheless, Europe understood the contextual and formal message of the film and honoured it with several prizes.

After *Sweet Emma, Dear Boebe* István Szabó made his next film only in 1996.

This was also an experiment. *Offenbach's Secret* was, for the most part, made in the town of Kecskemét. The atmosphere was provided by the stage of the town's late 19th century theatre, its boxes and many hidden nooks. It was shot with a high resolution television camera, but this new technical approach did not present a problem for Lajos Koltai. Using it he was able create the velvety shades and radiant halations so characteristic of him.

It happened in the 1990s that István Szabó returned to the genre of documentaries. The commission came from abroad, more precisely BBC Scotland asked him to present his home, Budapest or Hungary, as he himself wished. Lajos Koltai was able to present Budapest, the 'city of survival', as a living organism in the 56-minute *Steadying the Boat* (1996), while taking stock of the most important

In the Berlin Pergamon Museum Lajos Koltai measures the light on a symbolic character, The Thorn Pulling Boy in *Sunshine* (1998)

objects of the Szabó mythology, the clock, rucksack, the worn suitcase and the yellow tram. Koltai was free to move between documentary genres and he was free to make his remarks concerning the story line. However, that freedom was the freedom of a tight-rope walker high up in a circus. Nevertheless, it was the freedom he was used to in their joint work.

The comparison fits the film they made with the most demanding approach in the 1990s. *Sunshine* (1998) tells the story of three generations of Hungarian Jews in an otherwise unusually long, three-hour film. Among other challenges, Koltai had to utilise his special sensitivity to enable him to follow correctly changes in the characteristics of the Jewish way of life, in order to avoid the spectacle turning into a folkloristic depiction. The film caught his interest, as had *The Green Bird* two decades earlier. That has to be emphasised since in reality film making involves the resolution of daily tasks, and a battle and compromise with circumstances. In this situation it is mostly the director who must know the whole work by heart,

James Frain, Jennifer Ehle, Ralph Fiennes
(*Sunshine*, 1998)

The camera crew
prepares a shot at the
most characteristic
location of *Sunshine*

provided he is able to. However, Lajos Koltai has been able to become an outstandingly important creative partner for István Szabó because he also keeps the whole work in mind, and not only as the totality of images. They agreed that *Sunshine* was going to be a synthesising film, which would use strong images to show that truth has many sides. Commitment to the motherland has several reasons, which cannot be revoked by either the loss of values or political exclusion. The images had to reflect the tendencies of cultural self-expression in the 20th century. Thus the colours and lights had a dramaturgical function. They had to move from the intimate brown of family dinners to the cold of neon lights in the 1950s. The film, which Koltai shot with love throughout, brought him the award of the European Film Academy. He was happy, since the prize was an important argument for the cameraman's Europeanness in the dispute which denounced the film for being 'American'. What critics meant was that the film presented situations the viewer could identify with, a real line of thought. It also used outstanding actors like Ralph Fiennes.

This synthesising production did not block the way for further experiments. However, István Szabó was not able to make his film *Taking Sides* (2001) in Hungary (the Hungarian quotation was not competitive with the offer of Germany's Babelsberg). *Taking Sides* presented a difficult task for the cameraman. Ronald Harwood's drama is a gripping chamber play involving the clash between an American major and the conductor Wilhelm Furtwängler in the ruins of Germany in 1945. The major, who is deeply affected by the spectacle of the death camps, is leading an investigation into the case of the artist, who had continued with his conducting during Nazi rule. He is looking for the correct way to 'take sides'. Music lovers have no doubt that such a major talent, the best interpreter of Beethoven's music, cannot be responsible for Nazi rule. But the major does not think he can absolve anyone just because they are regarded a cut above the ordinary people making up the population. Koltai explores the taking sides issue utilising facial close-ups. There are more close-ups in *Taking Sides* than in any other Szabó film. But the faces of the two actors, Harvey Keitel and Stellan Skarsgård, could manage the close-ups. The story moves ahead even when they are silent.

The argumentative drama is made tense by having a basic tone again for the first time since *Confidence*. Cold blues and mouldy greens make the film analysing the relationship between artist and dictatorship especially awkward. Szabó and Koltai made no secret of saying that *Taking Sides* incorporated not only a historical lesson but experienced reality, since Hungary had censored film production for forty years. The language, themes and ways of expression had to be found under those conditions to enable the artist to avoid being a propagandist.

"RAISE HIGH THE ROOF BEAM"

In 1994 Lajos Koltai was unable to refuse another Brandauer commission. He was curious as to what could become of such a famous novel as Thomas Mann's *Mario and the Magician*. However, he also knew that Brandauer, who was to be the director and also play the main character, Cipolla, took on too much. Koltai actually was hesitant about that burden, too. Then the plan was suddenly dropped and what may be more important is that he could have made an American film. Stanley Kubrick called him to London to talk about a film, though he, of course, gave little information about it, expecting his colleagues not to deliberate on the task but take on a job in his films out of unlimited and unconditional adoration of his greatness. However, the film in question was not made because Kubrick is thought to have discovered a similarity of theme with Spielberg's *Schindler's List*, the rushes of which were first seen by him. Lajos Koltai still thinks today that to work with Kubrick would have been the great experience of his life, although without doubt his fame and his infamous whimsicality may have crumpled Koltai. Nevertheless, without having made the film Koltai can still refer to the title of a novel by the favourite writer of his generation, J. D. Salinger – "Raise High the Roof Beam".

In 1994 Brandauer waited for Lajos Koltai to be free and in the meantime relocated his story from southern Italy to Sicily due to its longer summer. But the careful choice of location was to no effect. The film mostly fizzled out because of the actors. Brandauer's performance lacked the demonic touch which had characterised the theatre performance by Zoltán Latinovits, who represented the model for Koltai. During shooting there were constant arguments between director and cameraman, though even Koltai felt that his cinematography would not be able to save the film. He was right. Some basic tone is present in most of the film. The outlines are elusive and pastel shades are dominant; the interiors and exteriors are finely tuned and the atmosphere when the family of the writer (Thomas Mann) arrives at the hotel is the peak of cinematography. Even the extravagantly lit finish could not have been criticised had the plot support it a little. Koltai learnt much from the film, primarily about dramaturgy and how a director's wanton

A crew photograph again: as the background immediately indicates, taken on the last day of shooting *The Legend of 1900* (1998) in Odessa

FACING PAGE: Hell – the inside of the ship (Tim Roth)

interventions can ruin literary material. (For example, it is not Mario who shoots Cipolla, rather he is killed by his lover Silvestra. Why? The film does not give an answer since new contexts or viewpoints cannot be discovered as a result of the change.)

Nevertheless, Italy attracted Lajos Koltai. It was an Italian director, Giuseppe Tornatore who asked him to film *The Legend of 1900* (1998). In 1989 Tornatore had directed *Cinema Paradiso*, which became a cult film, winning an Oscar in the foreign films category. Undoubtedly he is a director attracted to stories reflecting fables and legends, and there is always a child or an adolescent in the centre who learns about the world primarily via an adored woman. The way he contracted Koltai was also a legendary event. Dante Spinotti, Tornatore's former cameraman, suggested Koltai, though he had not met him, just knew his films. Thus Koltai got in touch with the director and as Tornatore relates the story he immediately knew that the Hungarian was going to film *The Legend of 1900* after they had looked into each other's eyes at their first meeting. His decision was wise. What was required for the biggest Italian film production of the 1990s was a cameraman toughened on American super-productions like *Mobsters* or *Just Cause*. The story of the baby left on an ocean liner becomes 'believable'

because it is on the borderline of reality and fable, though the theatrical composition did not help here. Lights had to create the image of floating which divides the story into different units. Shooting was hell, not only because Tornatore's demands squeezed the maximum out of everyone but also, for example, the interior of the Odessa boat with its 'inferno' was built exactly on this association, while the 'above' symbolised luxury and heaven. Lajos Koltai used plenty of innovations in both locations. For example, for the first time he used motion control, a computer-assisted technique which is able to repeat the most complicated camera movements. And there were complicated movements, for example, a 'dance' of the piano in a sea storm, when many different movements had to be coordinated and resolved successfully several times. The difficulties of cinematography were increased because the director was mostly thinking in terms of long takes to achieve atmospheric unity and decided on cinemascope, which resulted in the surroundings being seen even in the close ups. Therefore they had to be lit with the same care as in the places requiring long shots. Koltai's pictures managed to convince the director, who seemed to forget good manners during shooting, that they were on the right track, and of course he was not alone because the camera crew was put together by Dante Spinotti, a sign of incredible respect for a colleague.

The deck – Heaven (Melanie Thierry)

FACING PAGE: Monica Bellucci (*Malena,* 2000)

In 1999 Lajos Koltai was at the peak of his career. He received the Europe Prize, the highest award of the European Film Academy for the cinematography of the films *Sunshine* and *The Legend of 1900* in Berlin on 4 December 1999. In a carefully made interview given at the time he said: "It is still the picture which is the continuously speaking language of film. And it will continue to be more so. I think that pictures speaking for themselves have to be composed instead of dialogues." He also described Tornatore's character and directorial style: "Despite the fact that he knows everything, he keeps it a secret until the day we start the scene. It is then when the secret has to be revealed. So much surprise is needed."[12] Let us not forget this sentence, because here Koltai made a confession about his own method of work using Tornatore as an excuse.

[12] Nagy, Elisabeth (reporter): *1999 Európa-díjas operatőre: Koltai Lajos* (Europe Prize Cameraman of 1999 – Lajos Koltai). *Filmkultúra, Arcok,* 1999.

FACING PAGE:
Annette Bening
(*Being Julia,* 2002)

Giuseppe Tornatore thought that in view of the prizes it would be silly to change the winning team and was willing to wait for Lajos Koltai. The new film was *Malena* (2000), the story of a young woman with an erotic attraction who goes through a heavenly and an infernal experience during World War II. An important role was that of a thirteen-year-old adolescent, who is also scorched by the Sicilian woman's beauty. The adolescent and the cameraman became friends. The boy felt that there was a man in the crew for whom he was not only a character but also a personality and with whom he could converse in English. Tornatore's story line involved a special difficulty in terms of the cinematographic approach. The story is told by the adolescent in later life – the psychological processes are broken into mosaics, while the two time scales must always be identifiable. The mythical effect is generated by a plenitude of colour and black and white pictures filled with the irony of reality and fantasy. Influenced by that, we are inclined to accept the behaviour of ordinary people as ageless, as well as the continuously repeated myths. Koltai persevered but he could not easily accept that the director, when he did not see exactly what he had imagined, as is usual, looked for someone to blame. But when Koltai accidentally fell into his vision he immediately signalled to him not to misunderstand, he was not blaming the Hungarian cameraman. However, Tornatore could not have known then that Lajos Koltai would be elected a member of the Society of American Directors of Photography, nor that the American Academy of Motion Picture Art and Science was going to nominate him for an Oscar for achievement in cinematography, with respect to the film *Malena*.

Certifying Lajos Koltai's Academy Award nomination for Best Camera Work in *Malena* (2000)

The difficulties of shooting were increased by Tornatore's decision to film in Morocco, because having travelled through Sicily to find the world which characterised the island before he was born he thought Morocco was more like the former Sicily than the present, even most hidden part of the island. With this he added to the psychological burden of being close together. Yet Koltai had special means to cope with the difficulties. When he could he locked the door of his room and read a novel. He read slowly, weighing up each word and thus he 'consumed' a daily portion. He was careful to make the book last until the end of filming. Simultaneously, he increasingly thought that a new chapter was going to start in his life.

THE STORY OF FATELESS

THE BOOK AND THE WRITER

The book Lajos Koltai was reading during the lonely hours while filming *Malena* was the novel *Fateless* by Imre Kertész. Having read the first pages he already felt that he had been struck by the light Saint Paul had seen on the way to Damascus. This story of torment during the Holocaust becomes especially painful in the novel by it not presenting a prosecutor; consequently there is no accusation and no judge, and thus no sentence is passed. Those who executed the most horrible genocide of the 20th century are so-called normal people. Lajos Koltai had known that the Holocaust stood out among historic crimes. However, only these pages made him finally conscious that the story was also really *ours*. He realised what the book states with a shocking force – let us not think that the story can be finished by counting the dead, bowing our head and apologising. Those who remained alive are also losers – their fate, which provided a framework for and gave sense to their lives and existence, has been taken away. Furthermore, the angle of the "big boy in the fifteenth year of his life" provided additional surprises. In contrast with some 'compulsory' components of similar stories, this description makes the Holocaust horrible by lacking atrocities. The machinery can hardly be seen, since organisation is not yet a conceivable reality for a child. Rather the elementary need for human relationships is emphasised, and that is what adults usually forget.

Already in the opening pages, when the father's forced labour 'procurements' are being organised, Koltai saw a deeper meaning in the rucksack and other objects ensuring survival in the István Szabó mythology, and about which the mother could talk with so much emotional emphasis in the film *Budapest Tales*. The viewer should not look for the scene of 'procurement' in the film. It was not included in the screenplay, but Koltai had read the novel.

He got under the spell of its world, which brought to the surface and mobilised what he had known of the Holocaust, and he put every bit in proper order as the law of nature requires, just like a strong magnet does to metal shavings. He immediately sensed that a child's angle allowed reality to be interpreted with an enlightening force. He thought long about what the first person singular meant in the novel. What does it mean that Gyuri Köves 'solves' the anti-Jewish hatred of the baker, who, in his opinion, would not be able to cheat on the Jews if he did not hate them, that is, if this were not a concept governing his action, "which of course may involve something quite different". The linguistic form of the writing, however, made it clear that the writer firmly stood between Gyuri Köves and the reader, and he does not let the reader conceive the story as a melodrama out of either sympathy or love for the child.

Lajos Koltai read the book slowly (itself a recommended mode of discourse with *Fateless*) and was thinking for days about the meaning of Gyuri Köves's response after the slap on his face that made his nose bleed. The book says: "…But still, I was very mad, because I was not yet used to being hit by anyone, and so, by my sitting and by my gestures I tried to give a strong vent to my anger. He must have noticed this, I think, because I saw that, even though he kept on shouting, the look of his dark, almost oily eyes gradually began to soften and then finally became an almost apologetic expression. During this time he studiously examined me from head to toe. Somehow I had an uncomfortable, tense feeling."

Did the absurd apology flashing in the eyes of the prisoner in a black riding suit really happen, or was the explanation of Bandi Citrom, the homosexual with a patchouli smell, correct? Of course, Citrom did not give an explanation about the look but about the man in the black suit as a phenomenon. Did Köves at that moment of humiliation seek the possibility of forgiveness and thus did the apologetic look only exist for his own contemplation?

Then, in contrast, the end of the book with Gyuri's arrival home, his hatred extending to everything, and "the happiness of the concentration camps" made Koltai ponder most. He immediately felt that this was not an isolated reflection; every reader must engage in that, otherwise they would not understand what living and constituting someone else's fate meant. Periods cannot be cut out of time and treated as if they had never happened – perhaps that is the book's emphasis.

Koltai had noticed earlier that he was taking the book to read in enclosed spaces. He realised, too, in Morocco that the remark of Camus, that lover of African sunshine, was absolutely correct: "Houses on the hilltop, gold in sunshine in a foreign country. It touches one emotionally more than the same spectacle at home. It is not the same sun."[13]

No, Lajos Koltai did not want to divert his attention with the sights of a foreign country. He wanted to be at home with the book, and he felt he was entirely at home within those four walls. The idea nested stubbornly in his head that *Fateless* was a special novel because it did not fall into the trap of most 20th century novels, including Jorge Semprun's masterpiece, *The Long Voyage,* which wipe out the borderline between reality and fiction. Koltai thought that Imre Kertész had focussed on the story of how a person was brought up, as reflected by certain classical writers, for example Goethe, which is a deeply personal story, but which nevertheless could perhaps be a starting point for a film.

It cannot be claimed that Koltai was reading the book 'innocently', for his own purposes. A young producer, who had worked with Péter Gothár, gave him the novel in Budapest saying that he had the film rights, that work had been going on concerning the book but that nobody liked the screenplay. Should he be interested, they could talk about it. Of course, the producer did not chose Koltai by chance. He knew the cameraman would like to prove his skills as a director.

A rather big storm was raised in professional circles since Koltai already had the cast and money to shoot another film, but he had the strength to say no to that because the writer suspiciously insisted 'filming' even his conjunctions. Koltai knew precisely that a film was not like literature and if the writer did not trust him the matter should not be forced. György Illés approved of his decision and fully supported his pupil's plans to direct.

[13] Camus, Albert: *Noteszlapok* (Notebooks). Bethlen Gábor Publisher, Budapest, 1993. p. 39

Arriving home after filming *Malena*, Koltai immediately started to investigate the writer of the exceptional novel. He was lucky in that a collection of short stories, *The Union Jack*, by Imre Kertész had just been published. It is an excellent 'introduction' to the writer's oeuvre, also in the context of film since, for example, the short story, *The Tracer*, could be particularly suitable for filming.[14]

Koltai wanted to meet the writer as soon as possible, since he read in the above story that "time was a dangerous enemy" and he agreed entirely. However, he learnt that he would have to wait because Kertész was working on his new novel in Berlin and when he was at home he was not into social life. Of course, there are always exceptions. Zsuzsa Radnóti, widow of István Örkény and the dramaturg of the Variety Theatre, held a 'literary salon' for selected participants, including Imre Kertész, who was greatly respected by connoisseurs in Hungary. Relying on their long acquaintance, Koltai asked Radnóti to arrange a meeting with Kertész purely so he would be able to meet the writer of *Fateless* in person. It took place at the next gathering of the 'salon'. The hostess appreciated Koltai's interest and sat him next to the writer. Thus they could speak to each other without any mediators.

"Today I skipped school. That is, I went, but only to ask my teacher to excuse me from class."
(The screenplay is the source for the quotations.
We did not think a caption necessary for all the pictures.
Following the spirit of the film, speech relies on the spectacle.)

[14] The dialogues in *The Tracer* infused Lajos Koltai's fantasy so much that later on he had the idea, which was then discarded, to make *The Tracer* the 'framework' for *Fateless*. Of course, the idea ended like all the other 'dramaturgically centred' concepts; all the apparently pleasing approaches proved to be weak compared to the natural flow of the novel.

LAJOS KOLTAI TO BE THE DIRECTOR OF FATELESS

Koltai was intoxicated with happiness after the meeting. The writer surpassed all his expectations since Kertész's exceptional personality lacks the kind of icy breeze which paralyses the surroundings of many 'great individuals', albeit perhaps unintentionally. In turn, Kertész also saw some hope in his acquaintance with Koltai, who had surprised him by analysing *Fateless* not only enthusiastically but also understandingly. He told him what the book represented for him and what an experience it had provided. Then he discussed how some parts of this high level literature could be translated into the language of film, utilising the composition of images and colour. Koltai drew the attention of the small group to himself. Several remarked that it would certainly be worth his while struggling with *Fateless*. Kertész could hardly utter a word. "I am blushing," he said, because like an adolescent he was embarrassed by all the praise, which he nevertheless could feel was not due to politeness but genuine conviction.

The word 'struggling' was deliberate. Over the years Kertész had been called on by several directors, including Americans, with the idea of filming *Fateless*. All had been unsuccessful, although Kertész did not in principle reject the idea of a film adaptation. The many reports about and interviews with the writer after he received the Nobel Prize made it clear that he did not look down on the cinema as was the case with many in his profession. Rather he liked films, believing that in the 20th century cinema had had the greatest effect on our way of life and even on how we reflect about ourselves and our everyday experiences.

However, when Kertész and Koltai first met *Fateless* was 'reserved', but the script, which had just been completed, with György Spiró participating as consultant[15] with a friend's devotion, did not satisfy the writer. But in order to be absolutely sure he asked the enthusiastic Koltai to read this version and since he was saying such positive things about the novel he could give his opinion about the screenplay.

Thus it happened that in Kertész's apartment the two of them began dissecting the novel, without pulling any punches. Koltai's enthusiasm did not subside and very soon they were discussing the principle idea of the story. In a cinema context the biggest difficulty of *Fateless* is that it is such a linearly developed story lacking in spectacular turning points, and each episode with its own special rhythm proceeds towards the dénouement, which, however, represents everything but a resolution, unlike in traditional, problem-raising plots. Steps must be made on the way and they are never long steps.

Imre Kertész and Lajos Koltai also agreed that longs steps and spectacular plots were already known. Holocaust depictions usually contain these spectacular momenta, with the aim of awakening the conscience of the audience. Consequently, the 'long steps' have become almost stereotypes and viewers are well familiar with

---

[15] Who wrote this version? Even those who themselves took part in it could not decide, since the title page of the screenplay said the following: "Written by György Spiró in the company of Imre Kertész."

ABOVE: "Who dares to confront so much youth, freedom and so much innocence?"

BELOW: The main character, the boy (Marcell Nagy) in the father's workshop

It is no routine task for Lajos Koltai to obtain the main character's best reaction, even after "long sessions" with the children; pictured here analysing patiently

From the boy's perspective we see the father handing over the workshop to his assistant, Mr Sütő

them. The story line of these types of films is actually accumulative: the behaviour of the Germans and the increasingly harsh and horrible treatment are focused on, which if the aim is to be authentic will either remain in the world of documentation or go astray towards absurdities via arbitrarily managed fantasy. Lajos Koltai also mentioned that the exterior story with all its pain and horror is only a background as compared to the story happening in the soul. Gyuri Köves's fate does not point towards the Holocaust, but since at the beginning of the story he is taken off a bus accidentally, his fate is taken away from him. Would not many people be threatened today if their fate were taken away unexpectedly? That is why the story is relevant.

This interpretation questions the traditionally perceived purpose of plot, since neither the question of getting into it nor getting out of it are raised, because what we see is history's 'joke'. It forces the boy to have a different fate from what he would have had. "I have nothing directly to do with the Holocaust, which I naturally condemn deeply, but if I had to adapt the novel to a film I would not try to pronounce a final say about the Holocaust. It would be enough to show a human story." Lajos Koltai could have said something similar in a nutshell, as much as the two parties from different angles remember the themes of a long talk.

Presumably Kertész was affected by Koltai not only accepting the linear nature of the story line but considering it a principle characteristic. The person who imagines the novel as a film must be aware that loss of humanity is the drama, while the road leading to the Holocaust is not paved with major twists, in contrast to what we traditionally tend to think. The writer did not smile at such ideas expressed by Koltai, but said: "Fantastic! I wrote exactly that." He stood up and went to the phone to ring the Hungarian producer, at that point Péter Barbalics, and told him that Lajos Koltai was going to direct the film.

When Kertész stated that Koltai was going to direct the film, the latter might have been shy out of feeling for his colleagues. But he was not. He had already thought for some time that the story and the book would enable him to appear before the world not only as a cameraman. And if his approach was liked by the writer, then he had no reason to retreat only because of formalities. Still it was not he who made the decision. Imre Kertész wrote a letter which made the situation clear in all respects.[16] He also announced his decision to the German producer who had 80 per cent of the filming rights at his disposal. The producer immediately came to Budapest to get further information about the background to the matter. Koltai also met him in the Viennese Café in Buda, where the would-be director unfolded at length how he would like to direct the film. At the end of the conversation the producer said he also understood why the writer wanted Koltai to adapt the novel to film, and that he had nothing against it but was actually pleased. Finally the film historians will also be pleased about the letter. The date of writing, 29 June 2000, exactly specifies the time when the story began.

---

[16] The letter has a history as we will see in the chapter *Conversation in Berlin with Imre Kertész about Fateless and the Cinema*.

THE YEARS OF PREPARATION

In handbooks about 'How to make a film' there is usually a chapter which is missing, one we might call 'The years of preparation'. This is actually not by chance. Everything seems so simple in the Hollywood system, which is the one regarded as authentic. Scriptwriters first make the 'hard' screenplay, and the producer then looks for a suitable director. The director not only receives a ready-made version, but also initials each page indicating he would direct only what is put down in writing. However, European films aspiring to an artistic standard are not made like that. Although many participate, there is only one maker: the director who 'creates' the film. How? Everyone does it differently, but it is sure that directing involves the art of communication. The director conducts a great number of conversations until the moment the sharp noise of the clapperboard signals the shooting of the first take. Lajos Koltai had the most important conversations with Imre Kertész. These discussions, even about those ideas which of necessity proved to be a dead end, placed the tiny details of the story in a new perspective and contributed to the director's comprehensive concept, which is often called the director's vision. This phase already showed that bringing the film together would involve a labour of Sisyphus. The German producer left at the end of 2001. He seriously explained to Lajos Koltai that the topic was not current in Germany and therefore the film would definitely be a financial flop should he finance it to the planned extent.

Meanwhile Koltai was completing his oeuvre as a cameraman. He made three films after 29 June 2000. One, immediately after *Malena*, was a 'college film', which takes place among the children of the American upper middle class. The *Emperor's Club*, directed by Michael Hoffman, depicts the clash between a teacher living under the spell of classical literature and an unscrupulous child (with his Congressman father behind him). The ending, highly appreciated by film critics, did not suggest American optimism at all.

Max was the next film. The two months of shooting this film began on 5 November 2001 and proved to be an opportunity that should not be 'missed'. On the one hand, András Hámori, the co-producer of *Sunshine*, offered it on a plate since he brought the production to Hungary to be filmed there. On the other, the Dutch director, Menno Meyjes, born in 1954, interested Koltai very much. Meyjes appeared on the scene as Spielberg's scriptwriter (*The Color Purple*, 1985), but he also participated in writing the script for Franklin J. Schaffner's last but one film, *Lionheart* (1987). Then he contributed to films by Spanish, Australian and French directors, prior to deciding it was time he himself directed his own screenplay. So Lajos Koltai was filming the unusual film of a late starter and first-time film director.

Max in the film is a fictitious character. Max Rothman (played by John Cusack) is an art dealer in Munich who lost an arm in the Great War. The downfall of the Empire does not prevent him from continuing to look for young talent, among them a certain Adolf Hitler (Noah Taylor) who has no family, home or friends. Max takes pity on him but unfortunately he directly tells the 'artist', who in the war rose only to the rank of corporal, that he is not gifted enough. Therefore, in

the fiction, Hitler feels compelled to seek a career in politics. Thus if Max had not been such a harsh critic the 20th century may have taken another turn.

In the shadow of *Fateless*, Koltai was not so much concerned about the absurd nature of the story (although it was difficult for him to get over it) but he attentively observed the efforts of the great master of the profession, Ben van Os, Peter Greenaway's scenic designer, and his Hungarian assistant Tibor Lázár, who had to transform Budapest into Munich at the beginning of the 20th century.

The film *Being Julia* is unusual in its genre. István Szabó adapted Somerset Maugham's *Theatre*, balancing between drama and comedy, and started shooting with his usual team, naturally including Lajos Koltai. The film, made in the summer of 2003, had an interesting cast which included Annette Bening and Jeremy Irons, but by then they were not so exciting for either Koltai or his director.

The test for them was presented by how easily they could move about in the intimate world of theatre after the large historical frescos, which film mythology often covered with a colourful gown. Yet they were not anxious. With the film *Offenbach's Secret* they had already tried out the basic location, the Kecskemét Theatre, which provided an authentic background to the story set in the 1930s.

Koltai worked with his usual devotion, but whenever he looked into the future *Fateless* appeared on the horizon and it is possible to say that his film was actually ready to begin.[17] The most important artistic factors, the cast and locations were

The family:
the stepmother
(Judit Schell),
the father
(János Bán)
and the boy
at their last lunch

[17] My conversation with Lajos Koltai in a lunch break during shooting *Being Julia* in Kecskemét at the end of June also proves that *Fateless* was ready in its outlines. Since there was a sort of competition concerning the 'shooting diary' of *Fateless*, I asked the question, with reference to an earlier promise of Vince Books, what if Lajos Koltai's career on the occasion of *Fateless* and a report about the film when it was being shot were published.

about to be finalised. The 'team' was also together – for example, while doing some additional shooting for *Max*, Koltai offered the job of scenic designer to Tibor Lázár, who, although surprised at first, agreed.

National attention revealed that the search for locations was intensive. For example, the local newspaper in the town of Dunaújváros reported on 20 March 2003 that Koltai had found an eerily faithful looking location in the buildings of the disused furnace where the Zeitz deportees worked. It is also known when Lajos Koltai first saw the main location of the film, where the Buchenwald concentration camp had to be reconstructed.

Having tracked down Koltai's telephone number, a member of the cultural committee of the Piliscsaba local authority rang him up and said: "I know you are looking for locations. I think the shooting range at Piliscsaba, which I want to show you, would be of interest."

Koltai believed the unknown caller, whose name merits recording. He was Jenő Platschek and he was concerned with the search for location in as much as nine members of his family were deported to Auschwitz. None returned.

Koltai visited Piliscsaba on 14 January 2003. Although the production plan originally involved reconstructing the camp at Szabadbattyán, both Koltai and Lázár immediately felt that the sandy area torn out of nature was Buchenwald. Imre Kertész was shocked when he saw photographs of the place. It was not the external factors but the quintessential similarity. Both at Buchenwald and at the disused shooting ground the place was strikingly an infected wound in nature. In Germany, for example, it is the wounded Buch woods, which used to be a favourite walking spot of Goethe when he happened to get bored with the bustle of Weimar.

THE SCREENPLAY

In the previous chapter we jumped a bit ahead in the sequence of events. Everyone knew that in order to shoot *Fateless* a screenplay and financing partners were needed. The screenplay was produced more quickly than the financial means. During the discussions Imre Kertész was the first to say that the work done on the script so far was flawed. Its main mistake was that it lacked emotions. He produced an example to illustrate this. The element of the child crying at the end of the day when they say farewell to the father was not depicted. What was missing was that the boy had felt obliged to meet demands all day. The important aspect, whereby the boy would like the father to leave for forced labour so that at least he would know that the boy had done something for him, was lacking in the script. For example, he prayed although he did not understand the words of the prayer. Briefly, Kertész said what otherwise Lajos Koltai had also thought of but did not want to enforce on the writer. He patiently let him discover the absence of emotions. His partner had little experience in filming but 'learnt' during the work

what the difference is between speech and vision, not theoretically but as a result of the nature of a film. Koltai also realised with a clever sensitivity that co-operation would be successful if he respected Imre Kertész as a writer. The writer must not be limited but rather freed from the burden of 'rules' which may be right in the rulebook of 'how to write a script' but not in the case of *Fateless*.

The obvious was agreed: let Imre Kertész write the screenplay, notwithstanding the fact that his former directors had advised against the use of voice over, whereas the strong surge of reflective monologue plays an important role in the dramatic effect of the novel. Kertész began work with pleasure and was quickly ready with the script, which was published in German and Hungarian. He regarded it important to write a preface to go before the script, though this did not appear in the Hungarian edition. I will rectify that, with Imre Kertész's permission.

"To write a screenplay by adapting a novel is a dangerous game; but it is sometimes more dangerous if the writer does not do it, since there are novels which cry out to be on the screen in time and the intention of doing this is as irresistible as their writing was in the past. In the end the author has to admit that instead of wasting time on further evasive manoeuvres it is best if he himself starts the work after some bitter experience, for example having read a 'film story', which a professional scriptwriter has made using the novel, albeit with the best of intentions.

"Of course it may not be the best decision. However, I decided on this course. Nevertheless, I cannot forget the rule of the genre, namely that a script, unlike a novel, is not written for eternity but for the film director.

Ambling upstairs in the stairway the boy meets Annamária (Sára Herrer), who, in another story, could be called his first love

Therefore it is my duty to warn the reader: in vain it is to look for linguistic radicalism, which characterised the original work, my novel *Fateless*. A film and a novel are two entirely different genres. While the novelist has to create his own full universe with the means of language, the scriptwriter only has the task to modestly hand over a blank cheque, so to say, to the director and his fellow workers so that they can fill it in with their art and knowledge.

A shot which had already appeared to Lajos Koltai while reading the novel – the father tries on his rucksack before forced labour

"On the other hand, I have been less restricted by the unbreakable rules of the genre. The novelist's freedom is different from the scriptwriter who is adapting a novel; and if the two happen to be the same person then he can have the noteworthy experience involving what we could call a rather pleasant type of split personality. As a scriptwriter the author suddenly notices that he is becoming more expansive and personal: now he can give space to certain biographical detail and memories, even stories which he discarded more strictly as a novel novelist.

"In this sense writing the script has undoubtedly proved a more entertaining job. However, I could not say that it was more satisfactory. I was working on the one for a few months, and for exactly thirteen years on the other.

As I have mentioned, a novel is a full universe, which has to stand on its own. But a script is merely an open possibility, mere 'literary material', which can only be revived by expressive faces, voices, camera movement and music, in other words, artistic means beyond language."

Imre Kertész perceived exactly that a screenplay was an absurd genre. On the one hand, a literary form must be used for something which is not exactly literature. On the other, even the best screenplay has a short lifespan. During filming it perishes page by page and line by line, and it will become at best immaterial, though from the viewer's perspective "compared to what?". Critics want to sound very professional when they state that a director 'ruined' the script or used it better than expected. Such critics think that their fantasy is somehow able to own some optimum of realising the script, and they compare the film with that. It is obvious that in so-called genre films there are many re-occurring motifs and 'originality' is created by the way the parts are connected and through the acting, although the latter matters to a more modest extent, since the stars are contracted to provide familiar images.

Imre Kertész utilised the freedom of not having to create a linguistically closed system. By alternating descriptions, dialogues and the voice over he did not want the "blank cheque" to mean that professionals working on the film would not know what their task was. This approach followed the strategy employed by Bergman with his scripts. Any member of the film crew reading it will gain possibly the best information concerning the film, information which may not be seen on the screen. For example, in the case of *Fateless* they must notice in the very beginning that emphases had been somewhat rearranged as compared to the novel. Thus the description of returning home is at least as important as the middle part of the story consisting of three asymmetric chapters, which the writer gave the title of *Scenes from the Nazi Concentration Camps*. At the beginning of this section the writer thought it appropriate to appoint the way of depiction in a short essay. He wrote: "We must state that we are not attempting to depict the Holocaust but to follow the way of the soul and this way will lead through the concentration camp universe. Even if we have to abandon the illusion of authenticity – because it is impossible to be authentic – we will attempt at least faithfulness, reticence and the dismal grandeur of simplicity, which we hope can be worthy with respect to the bereavement of millions."[18]

It also concerns the story of the screenplay that the majority of literary critics rebuked Imre Kertész in that the script was not the novel. However there were some who saw the point. Reviewing the German edition,[19] the renowned film critic Fritz Göttler not only quoted the above sentences but, having understood the potential poetics of the film, he outlined the following: "The boy is plodding along a side street. Bright summer morning. He is hot and tired. His rucksack is on his

---

[18] Kertész, Imre: *Sorstalanság. Filmforgatókönyv* (Fateless. A Screenplay). Second edition, Magvető Publishers, Budapest, 2003. p. 80. First edition, 2001.
[19] Kertész, Imre: *Schritt für Schritt. Drehbuch zum "Roman eines Schicksallosen"*. Suhrkamp Verlag, Frankfurt am Main, 2002.

Uncle Lajos, the religious relative (Péter Haumann)...

back. Now he stops at a square. He looks around, gets orientated. He sees a crumbly cinema. He makes his way towards it."[20] It is clear that Imre Kertész 'coded' into the script that he wanted the film version of *Fateless* to fit in the hundred-year-old process of cinema and that he does not disown Rossellini's *Germany, Year Zero* or Truffaut's *The 400 Blows*. The time for a post-modern version of the Holocaust has not yet come.

NOBEL PRIZE

On 10 October 2002, Hungary and the world learnt that the Swedish Royal Academy had awarded the Nobel Prize for Literature to Imre Kertész for his writing "which is an advocate of the individual's fragile experience against the barbaric tyranny of history". The prize made *Fateless* well-known in Hungary, too, since everyone wanted to know why, for the first time, a Hungarian writer had received the prestigious award. Such a storm of attention had not occurred in 1997, when Kertész received the highest Hungarian award for art, the Kossuth Prize. After reading *Fateless* the majority was somewhat ashamed why it had not done its best to learn about the great writer living among them, and therefore was satisfied to hear that the novel was going to be filmed. I repeat the majority, because there was an indignant or sometimes directly anti-Semitic

[20] Göttler, Fritz: *Die düstere Pracht der Unverziertheit: ein Drehbuch von Imre Kertész. Süddeutchse Zeitung*, 2003. 04. 07.

minority, which tried to discredit the writer, the novel and the plan to film it with time-worn slogans of the past.

The Nobel Prize undoubtedly affected the film plan benevolently. Imre Kertész publicised the future film in his own way, turning to public opinion but strictly avoiding turning to any authority. He appeared on television, often with Lajos Koltai, and he confirmed what had been obvious so far: the idea of the film had appeared before the Nobel Prize. The Nobel Lecture, which originally bore the title of 'Eureka', delivered on 7 December 2002 in Stockholm at the ceremonial meeting of the Swedish Academy 'sent a message' to Lajos Koltai. Kertész categorically stated that the "grey trap" of linearity represented the dramaturgy of *Fateless*.

"Instead of a spectacular series of tragic and great moments, Gyuri Köves had to go through the lot, which is depressing and provides little variety, just like life itself." The greyness of linearity, however, does not result in monotony, which is due to the incredible richness of detail.

"Linearity necessitated filling in the situations entirely. It did not enable me, say, to jump over twenty minutes elegantly, if only because the twenty minutes gaped before me as an unknown and frightening black hole, like a mass grave."

If the twenty minutes take place at the Birkenau ramp, then the reason must be revealed why those who remember it testify only about a short chaos. Imre Kertész realised that, in contrast with the topoi of Holocaust literature and films, this period was overshadowed by the inability to act, inertia and the shame of willingness to cooperate, and that was how he depicted it.

The message said that the attraction of *Fateless* should not be created by a formal approach but that moments like the above should lift it out of the vocabulary of

...persuades the boy to do something for the father, for example, pray

ABOVE: The Köves family's farewell dinner

BELOW: The stormy farewell of the optimistic neighbours, Mr Steiner (Ádám Rajhona),
Mr Fleischmann (György Barkó) and Mrs Fleischmann (Kati Lázár)

ABOVE: Grandfather (Vilmos Kun) says good-bye as if anticipating his son's fate

BELOW: "His tight hug was unexpected and I was somehow unprepared
for it after his words."

commonplaces, given that the Holocaust also has its lexicon of commonplaces. This will perhaps contribute to seeing things clearly and allow the possibility of "redemption and catharsis".[21]

All this was not new to the director. The questions of depiction were continuously raised during the long conversations, sometimes in a way such that antitheses were established, among them the most important being that 'the film should be emotional but never melodramatic'.

At that time Lajos Koltai often appeared before the public. For example, the Hungarian Cinema Foundation elected him president of its National Advisory Board (the ministry's imprimatur, however, was not given), and as such he was often asked about the situation concerning Hungarian films. With respect to that he said passionately the following

[21] Kertész, Imre: *A stockholmi beszéd* (Speech in Stockholm). Magvető Publishers, Budapest, 2002. pp. 14–15, 21.

The boy still regards
the scene as
a strange play

Lajos Koltai directs the
take as a character
by the family table

The mother
(Ildikó Tóth)
wants the boy
to live with her

– from the viewpoint of *Fateless*. "The other day I was asked where cinema was going. Nowhere. A film is for us to tell a story as effectively and emotionally as possible. We used to be able to do that. I would be pleased if we could use this often well-spoken language which has existed for a long time."[22]

During the preparations of the film, whose financing was proving difficult, he was testing that language.

The difficulty was presented by Lajos Koltai's purposeful demands. He stated on many occasions that he did not want to direct any film, he wanted to direct *Fateless*. In practice that meant that in choosing the locations, constructing the sets and creating the costumes he wanted to exactly follow the writer, who said that the illusion of authenticity had to be given up but faithfulness should be a rule.

THE IMAGES

To prepare a film involves working ten to twelve hours a day, which represents a severe intellectual and physical trial. In fact, a director has to cope with much more during the actual shooting. However, this was not a problem for Lajos Koltai – his experience showed he had excellent training for it. In addition he had a good eye

[22] Tihanyi, Péter: *A buchenwaldi naplementék* (Buchenwald Sunsets). Conversation with cameraman Lajos Koltai, the director of the film *Fateless*. *Hetek*, 3 May 2003.

for selecting those who would be at his side when filming. Nevertheless, it was his inner 'creative studio' which had to determine the style of images.

Documents were his starting point and it was natural for him to turn to documents when he wanted to increase the effect of a scene. Appropriate pictures covered his production room and the gloomy prints of an outstanding photographer, György Beck, added to the atmosphere.

The documentary character of the film was not an unknown quantity for Koltai. He had gained sufficient experience during his career to make a film as if it consisted of shots 'in situ'; of course, in black and white since the pictures suggest that the lack of colour characterises the pictorial language of the Holocaust. Then the originally documentary pictorial concept began to form, all the time with the acknowledgement that many were going to be disappointed. In vain do they expect the familiar Auschwitz images – they will not appear. Moreover, the images will not even be similar, although at the same time the authenticity of the depicted objective world will be obvious.

What happened is a 'very simple thing' for Koltai, but in reality it involves the deepest secret of the creative process. To the director of a 'seeing type' the novel suggested an image and pictures, which, according to him, started to be arranged slowly into a film. Those images implied a strength which can make the film stand on its own, a strength which would make even dialogue unnecessary. There is an effect without words and the story can still be followed. A fiction had to be dispensed with. People, not the survivors, do not know the Holocaust but they have an image in their mind, which is the result of the documents. They will go to the cinema with that in mind and call the film to account in relation to its authenticity. They must be made to forget their preconceptions right from the start, because according to the director the essence of *Fateless* is not a story of tribulation, which can be otherwise depicted in black and white. He thought that the coloured images must be modified to a certain extent because full colour would mislead the viewers. The images of the Holocaust in the viewer's mind must be concerted with the pictures of the film. In order to achieve that, the colour pictures have to appear as if they were black and white, without actually being so. In short, it must be a colour film which provides an image of black and white.

The film maker became doubtful – a film made according to the above may be similar to other Holocaust films. He himself will add to the number of documents and the viewer will shortly include it among the others. So Lajos Koltai turned to the novel again in order to get some reassurance. He could achieve a lasting effect if he tried to permeate the pictures with the poetry of *Fateless*. The pictures must be raised from the level of documents to a height where they will be able to captivate new domains of recollection. He had strange thoughts, like considering that the picture, which in this case represents a scene that is a series of takes, should be similar to a sculpture, as if he were moulding the statue of past events into lasting bronze. That is, of course, only a metaphor, but it can be achieved – the two dimensional picture can be turned statuesque with composition, lighting, performance and above all by providing viewpoints which can be 'walked around' during editing. To resemble a statue does not necessarily mean something is static.

Sculpture must primarily be created in the head and not realistically on the screen.

Beauty became the cornerstone of the concept, which is strange in this context. We can even say it was a daring decision. Although *Fateless* is literature in every sense of the word, that is not what immediately comes to mind. Lajos Koltai

decided that during filming he was going to find authentic images which were appropriate for the beautiful, human story, to weave images on to the milestones Imre Kertész had outlined.

The milestones could be called the 'stations of a way of the cross' and then it will be clear why the consecutive pictures are groups of statues. Here the calvary consists of small steps. One first begins to starve, then be cold, later lice will envelope the body, there is death, but there is resurrection without the shadow of profanity falling on the fate-stricken way of the cross.

Lajos Koltai pondered the question of images together with the shooting technique. He insisted on a Panavision camera whose optical parameters could produce anamorphic, wide-screen pictures. Why anamorphic pictures? Due to their size, they are "amazing and just right for film". If some, pedantically, remarked to Lajos Koltai that spectacular American films used that type of imagery he would shrug his shoulders. The technique in itself is independent from the users' ideology.

"This size makes it possible to compose strong pictures: to show the connection between nature, environment and man. Conversely, this size of imagery makes the narrowing of the space, the isolation around people absurd."

The spaciousness of the designed setting and the inhuman crowdedness of its details may keep the composition in constant movement. However, positioning close-ups in the elongated rectangle obviously requires more ingenuity than in the television form with which we are familiar, since there will be more space to fill with spectacle or cover up in order to narrow attention when a face is shown.

ANOTHER YEAR PASSES

Here we return to the shooting of *Being Julia*. Yet if filming *Fateless* had been realistic in the summer of 2003 István Szabó would have respected his fellow film maker's independent task as director.

But *Fateless* was not yet ready for production – the story takes place in winter and Koltai insisted on the natural colours and lights of winter. In addition, the financial means were not as secure as the optimistic producer was implying. The total shocked everyone: the budget, which exceeding two billion forints, seemed in Hungary to be as high as Mount Everest. The budget, however, was not high because of the fees of actors and other participants. The cost of the settings to be constructed and the number of extras seemed to be extraordinary, what with the supplementary costs of costumes, transport and reserving locations. Yet, Koltai insisted on authentic settings.

"It cannot be expected even of most experienced actors that they will stand before a blue curtain and believe, moreover make believe, that a concentration camp is behind them. And to expect a child, on whom most depends, to do so is even less likely." Such was his argument with those who wanted to reduce the budget by curbing the spectacle.

The main argument, however, was that in lieu of faithful settings he could do nothing else but rely on the viewers' knowledge of the Holocaust, the images from which he would like to free them in the spirit of the novel. As was expected, Koltai was accused of megalomania and the arrows of malice rained down on him, but he did not mind – he had complete confidence in his concept.

More important things mattered to him – for example, the cast. As a former documentary cameraman he could have considered, in view of the age of the boy and his amateur status, employing amateur actors in the supporting roles, in order to make the boy's situation easier. Such actors could externally depict the characters well but would not overshadow the main hero. Yet he discarded the idea – the characters surrounding the boy will not only have to appear in the short time they appear, but also bring to the surface the matter of fate, and that is an actor's task. Nevertheless, casting did not have ready made solutions. Koltai rather looked for which features existed but were somewhat hidden in his actors, which he was ready to bring to the surface.

Without doubt, the most difficult task was to find Gyuri Köves. Koltai was fortunate in that he was able to call in the four thousand candidates from a previous casting selection. To his surprise many would have been quite suitable for

The boy cannot suspect yet that kissing the hand is of a decisive nature

ABOVE: The last seconds of innocence

the role, albeit with some compromise. However, he was patient. He waited for the 'right' boy to appear. And the day came.

Then a long operation began by working with a relatively large group of people so that the chosen candidate, Marcell Nagy, would not learn that he was going to be Gyuri Köves. The understandable reasoning was that he did not want anybody, including the boy, to make preparations for the role. The idea was that he would accept instructions only from the director, who had to win the boy's confidence during the rehearsals called 'sessions'. Lajos Koltai, who must have been a teacher in a previous life, succeeded in doing this. In addition, he knew he had to shield the chosen child from media attention. The child in a perfect intellectual condition should not be exposed to the exhausting demands of being a star, even if the aim was kind-hearted. The time will come for that. But the time was not clear at that point, since financing the film and consequently the start of filming changed from day to day.

Choosing the cameraman was nearly left to the last minute. A British name was raised but Koltai made a brave decision. He chose Gyula Pados who began shooting his first Hungarian feature in October 2002, *Control*, which he could regard as his personal success. That film was made with director Nimród Antal, who graduated from the Academy in 1995.

Pados had graduated as a cameraman from the Academy of Film in 1997 as Gábor Szabó's pupil, but he had primarily worked in Britain. Moreover he had shot a feature film there (*Hotel Splendide*, directed by Terence Gross). Koltai asked him just at the time when he and an advertising film-maker friend, Péter Bergendy, were preparing a film version of a Hungarian bestseller, *Stop Mummy Teresia!* It was lucky that *Fateless* just fitted in between the two shooting periods of that film, so Pados was able to say yes.

A definitive manifestation of the stupidity of the always active ultra-Right in Hungary signalled that something had started despite the changing dates. Levente Szörényi, a former beat musician, stated in an interview that they should not build a death camp in the Pilis Hills because it is a sacred place, "a special gathering place for dead souls and the spirits of ancestry".[23] When asked by a journalist from the weekly *HVG* what he thought of some people wanting to protect the chosen 'sacred' location with a human chain, Imre Kertész said: "The news I have heard from you means nothing to me. To use the words of my favourite philosopher, Wittgenstein, it is a sentence without sense."[24]

Amidst the euphoria of Euroimage's decision (despite the still current cash difficulties), the first shooting day was set for 15 December 2003. The machinery plodding along could at last get into first gear and then begin moving as fast as circumstances would allow. Lajos Koltai also agreed that any further delay might endanger the seriousness of the matter, since there is a dangerous point in the preparation of a film when it may all come to a halt. No, that moment should not be reached.

[23] *A Pilis szakrális hely. Interjú Szörényi Leventével* (The Pilis Hills are a Sacred Place. Interview with Levente Szörényi). *Magyar Nemzet*, 28 August 2003. p. 14
[24] *Haláltábor-díszlet* (Death Camp Setting). *HVG*, 2 September 2003.

The boy is taken off the bus

The Expert (István Gőz) and the Unlucky Man (József Gyabronka) in the Customs House

"Suddenly a tram wedges itself into the rows and simply cuts the march in half."

The policeman (József Szarvas) who slowly suspects what he is giving a helping hand to

"WE HAVE STARTED!"

15 December 2003.[25] The first shooting day generated enormous interest. The location of the scene is Wesselényi Street. It is the father's workshop in the cellar where the Christian Mr Sütő takes over the shop from the boss, who has been called up for forced labour. Will it turn out to be a double-edged opportunity? The anti-Jewish laws of the time were perceived by many as an opportunity for acquiring even the most modest Jewish property, while others – they were fewer – agreed to formally take over a business as a way of getting round the law. Mr Sütő is very willing, perhaps too willing. He would even give a receipt for the handed over valuables.

That something is wrong is crystallised in the stepmother's single suspicious sentence: "Shouldn't we have accepted the receipt from him anyway?" Judit Schell's suspicion is spot on, as is János Bán's reply: "What for? What's the point of a receipt when the legal authority robs you legally?"

The novel contains only a passing reference to such a dialogue. Imre Kertész himself made the dialogue 'sound' in the script. Seeing the two people, however, makes the written sentences life-like. Bán, who has performed mostly grotesque characters in recent years, conjures out of his irregular features the character of the eternal loser, for whom Gyuri must do something. The basis of the over-anxious willingness on the part of Mr Sütő, played by György Gazsó, is completely unknown at the beginning of the film. However, the real motive of his behaviour is soon going to be disclosed, albeit that the 'resolution' of his fate will only turn out at the end.

Lajos Koltai makes a noteworthy remark about Mr Sütő at the end of the shooting day. "I wanted Mr Sütő to let himself go emotionally. That is how Imre Kertész wrote it. The scene should be almost a pretend play for the boy. Mr Sütő bursts out crying so compassionate he is, but he only feels sorry for himself and that is why he is weeping. Let the scene turn into self pity and let the child look numbly through the glass at what is happening. His stepmother also weeps, so does Mr Sütő and only the father is strong and self-aware. He clearly sees his own situation. It is absolutely necessary to take the scene like this, so that later it will be clear why Mr Sütő says: "Madam, do not be so remote from me." The sentence will have to be remembered when the Fleischmanns tell the boy that the stepmother had gone with a Mr Kovács or Futó or, of course, with Sütő. When the story will be told in full, this thread will also be unravelled.

16 December 2003. The Köves family live in an apartment at 21 Andrássy Road, whose elegant street façade is still preserved by a foreign institution. The scene

---

[25] At this point we begin to follow events 'step by step'. Jottings made during the fifty-nine shooting days comprise several thick notebooks. However, we will try to pick the more important pages, since it is obvious that a script will come to nothing after filming and that is even more true for the fate of a diary after shooting. Then it is only the film which stands up for itself.

actually only shows the staircase, the corridor and the room looking to the courtyard, from where the staircase can be seen. It will be a difficult day because the boy has to perform scenes which take place at four different times. Yesterday he only had a 'taste' of his role – he had to observe the adults' behaviour. It was enough for us to see that he sees through them. However, he is the main character today. He bumps into Annamária in the staircase. Gyuri has to be emotional in the scene since the girl is not indifferent to him. That is the surface. The deeper context will also only turn out at the end of the film. There is a rhyming pair – since there will be another meeting at this place. The 'sound' is similar, but the content is just the opposite, and the contrast must penetrate the viewer's heart. Even so, the viewer does not know what has happened. In the darkness of the cinema it is sufficient to have the feeling of déjà vu.

The question is inescapable as to why they do not also film the final staircase scene, since, if not, the crew will have to move into the building again in the future. But there is a psychological obstacle. Lajos Koltai considers that if he overturns the time sequence of the 'step by step' process in the boy, the process of horror appearing in his eyes will be lost. The child does not have to pretend he is Gyuri Köves but during the sixty days of shooting with his healthy mind he must believe himself to be Köves, albeit he is fortunate enough to have an other life, today in 2003.

Still, the sequence of time turns over. The scene is followed by an episode which takes place two months later in the script. Gyuri Köves is going on the corridor towards their flat. The script says: "He is stronger than when we last saw him, his face is suntanned." By the time the boy is before the camera everything is as instructed. For Kati Jakóts, the brilliant make-up artist, this was child's play. It also suits the sporty boy's age and constitution. That the episode is only the beginning of the scene with Mr Sütő and the stepmother will only turn out later.

17 December 2003. Shooting at night in the Mafilm studio. Tibor Lázár has condensed all the rooms of the Köves flat into one set. Kertész's script gives only

Does the policeman really encourage him to flee?

While rehearsing, the cameraman, Gyula Pados,
and the director turn up in the march

this description: "A somewhat stuffy, petit bourgeois flat with characteristic furnishings of the period. Oversized pieces of furniture, crochet doilies, knick-knacks, a round dining table, a glass cabinet with a characteristic clock on top, which strikes the quarter hours with the sound of Big Ben, etc."

The furnishers translated this into reality – as if passing a high-level exam on the knowledge of style and objects. Still, there is a discussion. Regarding the objects, how many are too many and how much is sufficient? How can the oversized furniture accommodate the free movement of the camera, the lighting, and so on?

The 'sensation' of the night is Imre Kertész's 90-minute visit to the set, accompanied by a number of journalists. The writer was surprised to see his sentences come to life – the mass of objects he had not seen since childhood. While chatting to a journalist he said: "I admire Koltai's vision. I expect the director to make the film surprise me just like anybody else. I handed him the script as a blank cheque. It is up to him to fill it in."

Koltai only remarked: "It's fantastic how Imre Kertész trusts me. I can use the novel freely. Imre actually encouraged me not to try to rewrite the novel as a film, which would anyway be in vain, but attempt to translate it into the language of imagery."

The "human transport" is crowded into the courtyard of the gendarme barracks. They are first robbed and their identities are taken away

This attempt is being conducted on the set at night due to difficulties with the cast's other engagements. Koltai definitely knows that the scene is extremely important. If he can pin the viewer to the chair now, he will have a good chance later to be able to get near his heart, too. The scene must not evoke the feeling of some kind of Jewish 'last supper'. According to the spirit of the novel, from the boy's perspective the get-together is grotesque and tragic at the same time.

What characterises the family in the director's early concept? "Sentences, unnecessary importunities, solicitous eyes, interrupted, angular and unfinished motions, fragile, mosaic-like, a little dim and slipped, almost slowed down still life pieces reflected in a mirror."[26] Today this 'still life' must be created from mosaics and takes.

19 December 2003. Judit Schell and János Bán understand the director's concept, which Koltai willingly explains to everyone interested. He also expresses his intentions at the end of the day.

"This scene has a single suffering hero, the father who is leaving. The others around him perform. Moreover, it is a family performance they have already experienced on other days. That is mirrored by the accustomed gestures and individual acts. I have singled out three people from the family: we can say that their glances makes up the axis of the scene – the silent glances of the grandfather, father and the child. The father is watching his son all evening, just as the grandfather is watching him. He feels this man has been lost. The boy is looking at the father because he has embraced him for the first time and the boy does not know why. Moreover, he wants to comply with what is expected of him. Thus the whole thing is a performance, but there is a point which turns the ease of a performance around. This is when the father picks up the rucksack. I have been preparing for this take throughout the scene. The viewer must also feel the weight of the rucksack, not because of the actual weight but its function. The viewer must realise that this careful preparation is absolutely absurd, which he must already confront at the beginning of the film. János Bán's face in the frame expresses this to me, and it is worth more than any external, professional bravura."

In addition to the father and stepmother, we can witness rare acting performance in this scene. Péter Haumann has been excellent in the role of Uncle Lajos. Why did the director think of Haumann to play this role?

"I do the casting very simply. I imagine what the actor will look like when he takes his place on the set. I ask myself – can he actually exist in this setting? During the screen testing it became clear to me that no one else but Péter Haumann could assume the role. He is the only one who can make the boy pray. Uncle Lajos has faith, he is also wry, busy with his own things, but someone is needed in the family who can do it, since in the Köves flat nothing refers to religion playing any role in their life. Nothing, just as religion did not play a role in the Kertész family. There

[26] Koltai, Lajos: *Sorstalanság. Rendezői intenciók* (Fateless. Director's Intentions). 2002. Manuscript

ABOVE: At the end of their journey in the wagons the children spell an unknown place name – Auschwitz-Birkenau

BELOW: Life-saving advice, say "Sezcajn. Verstajst? Sezcajn!" (Géza Tóth)

The selecting officer (Sándor Zsótér) leaves his hands
on the boy's face for a moment

The most frequent
order: "Alle raus!
Fünferreihen! Los!
Bewegt euch!" German
professionalism at work

Cameraman Gyula Pados
setting the camera movement

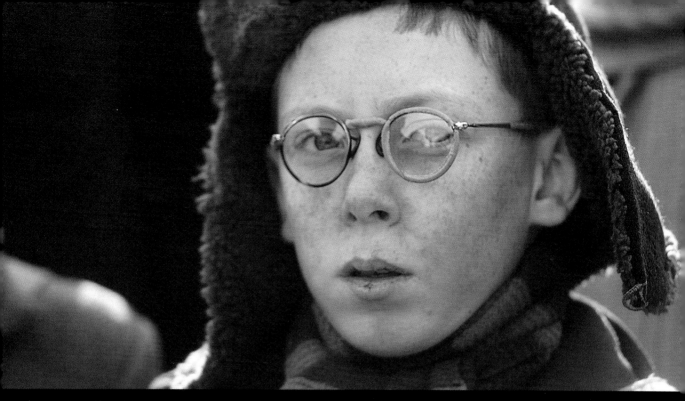

Whom the advice did not help; the little Moskovics (Dániel Szabó) was selected among those unable to work and we no longer see him

also, only the grandparents were religious. However, they did not force it on the children."

It also shows that Lajos Koltai imagined the scene in a studio from the very beginning, although it would be possible to find a petty bourgeois flat in Budapest satisfying the requirements and capable of being altered for the purpose.

"When I started my career I could not imagine shooting in a studio. 'Out to the streets, to free space!' That was the slogan we followed. I hated studios. I did not believe anything that was made in a studio. That must have been due to my inexperience. Today I can solve anything in a studio and in addition I am not at the mercy of the changes in outside light. I can work on a set continuously, even for fifteen hours. Of course the set should be such that when I make a bad turn I would knock my elbow, just like in a real interior. So the walls should be solid. It would not even occur to me to film through a wall a bed pushed to the wall. Today I like well-designed sets … If I think about how much exterior shooting we will do in winter then I can even say I actually like this old studio, where so many Hungarian films were shot in the past."

21 December 2003. A peaceful late autumn Sunday. The 'mild dissolution' of Budapest in 1944, as Imre Kertész's script says, must be shown in exterior. Naturally, this means the environment-ruining effect of the war years. The location, Lőrinc pap Square is very near the central building of the Academy of Drama and Film. We can ponder how many times Lajos Koltai crossed the square unaware that he will once use this small space in the VIIIth district where there is a blue-brick church. Koltai has good memories of the church. He was shooting the examination film *Silent Night*, directed by Tamás Farkas, which was about a novice, and some scenes were shot in the church. They made such good friends with the Jesuit priest at the church that they went back to drink the almond scented mass wine for a long time. Moreover Koltai's church wedding was celebrated by him in 1969.

Lőrinc pap Square is an important location. Here for the first time the viewer sees Gyuri Köves, who, with a canary yellow star on his chest, has to look up at the passers by, a bit defiantly and a bit in an embarrassed way. The boy must show this complex psychological state while the voice over, quoting the first sentence of the novel, says: "Today I skipped school. That is, I went, but only to ask my teacher to excuse me from class…"

Lajos Koltai keeps to his original idea, namely shooting in a chronological order, at least as far as he can.

"That is the only way I can make our Gyuri Köves pass along the stations authentically. But production matters must also be kept in mind. For example, traffic can only be stopped in the square on a Sunday."

People are looking for the director. They still do not want to believe that he has given up his place behind the camera to Gyula Pados. The explanation is witty. "If I were also the cameraman I would have to say to my actors that I will disappear during shooting. This would be the typical case of a hit and run

The Kollman children and their companions from Kisvárda give a performance in the barrack used for "theatre performances"

The director explains even to the extras what a "theatre performance" may be like here

Zeitz was a "smallish, poor, out of the way, one may even say provincial concentration camp"

Dusk sets in after a monotonous day of captivity

In rain, snow and with diarrhoea ▶

The boy in front of the latrine at dawn

accident. When the camera is rolling I must hold the actor's hand, especially in the case of Gyuri Köves. Of course, allegorically. But I must see his eyes from as near as possible, since the eyes cannot pretend. Eyes make a scene real or false."

"And the details," I could add. Lajos Koltai has the ability to pay the same attention to detail as to the whole. He has found an outstanding partner in the person of Gyula Pados who instructs his crew from the camera with equal awareness.

19 January 2004. Holidays have gone and we are well into January. Shooting continues today in Buda, in an elegant small street called Ág Street, leading up to Nap Hill. This is where Lajos Koltai and Tibor Lázár found the mother's flat. So it is a real flat which shows that Koltai is not dogmatic – a set could have been added to the studio complex but he did not do that, considering the atmosphere here more important than the handy services of the studio. He explains: "The intention was clear – to show the contrast between the father's petit bourgeois flat and the mother's elegant Buda apartment, which has a touch of debauchery. The only space in the flat was so clear that I immediately liked it. A flat which fully describes its resident. It is not big, so the mother's financial position is not the best either. Why build the apartment in the studio when it already exists? Incidentally, to build it well would have cost a lot. And I did not want to compromise. The reason why this flat is so vitally important is that the boy sets off for here in the end. After he has exhausted all his possibilities – Bandi Citrom has died, strangers have moved into their flat, the stepmother has married Mr Süto – he cannot go to anyone else but to his mother."

The scene depicts complex feelings again, primarily in the mother since she would also like the child to live with her and not the stepmother, once the father is on forced labour. The boy has to show that he is attracted to his mother, but he also has a kind of pride. He cannot move over to Buda because he has given his word. The scene must be powerful so that the viewer would remember it sharply all along. In the role of the mother, Ildikó Tóth must support that, but she cannot overpower the boy or become languid in order to make the child's acting easy. Managing the actors relies on the art of proportion. Koltai's concept is firm, the differences between the takes is minimal.

20 January 2004. Fateless is filmed in the studio again. The set of the *Köves* flat is entirely dismantled, the space is somewhat modified and by today it gives room to Annamária's "nursery furnished with a taste of the upper middle class". Tomorrow's set is also ready, the Fleischmanns' petit bourgeois flat, which is a little more age-worn and elderly looking than the Köveses. Talking about the flat, Koltai reveals an interesting 'secret': "Imre Kertész repeatedly told me not to make a kind of Anna Frank from Annamária. Of course, it is a completely different matter. Her parents do not care about her, therefore on the level of her thinking, she herself must face the meaning of wearing the yellow star. She does not have

A character in the camp: Bandi Citrom (Áron Dimény)

...who teaches the boy how to survive

And they even
feel like soaring
while drying

anybody to ask what it is. I tried to refer to that with the furnishings of the flat. There are only single portraits on the walls. There is no family picture. I do not think the viewer will notice that since I will not lay a large emphasis on the furnishing, but I hope that seeing the environment the viewer will have a notion of strangeness."

So today they have to depict the grown-up like conversation of a group of children with dramatic stresses. Annamária has the most difficult task, her stifled emotions suddenly come to the surface. Gyuri's response to this is especially important in the novel. This is the reason why *Fateless* can be called an ontological novel. Lajos Koltai must translate this ontological element into the children's gestures, tone of voice and the rhythm of their sentences. He does it. The almost Sisyphean work of auditioning the children and the 'sessions' are bearing a yield now. We are shocked to see Annamária's, that is Sára Herrer's excited gestures on the monitor showing what the camera is taking.

"A miracle," says Lajos Koltai, which at this moment not only means that the take was alright but he literally means it, since we have not witnessed an actor's routine performance or a self-exciting extremity but the human mind's helplessness against fate.

22 January 2004. I arrive at the Lórév Danube crossing, where today Koltai is filming one of the key scenes. It is about Gyuri Köves being taken off the bus by a policeman. What is feverish activity seems like nerve-wracking slowness. When everyone reports that shooting can start, Koltai puts his arm around the boy's shoulders and repeats patiently, with simple words, why the scene is important. This is when fates change – Gyuri Köves receives another fate instead of his normal one. From this moment on the Holocaust will become his fate.

The crew are dressed like Eskimos against the wind, which makes the temperature of minus six feel even colder. The colour green is absent in the sunlit landscape. I have already talked about a miracle. That is what we are expecting now. Here angels, who appreciate winter, may fly over. Angels are not accidentally mentioned – which of the many repeated takes will be the right one, what is the tiny difference which makes one exciting and the other boring can be stated by critics only afterwards. However, immediate response is required on location, during shooting, and after some time the director will say "we'll move on", because the most joyous moment – the miracle – has happened. It is worth moving a huge machinery called *Fateless* for such a moment.

Incidentally, Lórév is the first location where there is time to 'feel at home'. Shooting takes three days, including Saturday, and it mainly takes place in the Customs House setting, the location of seven consecutive scenes. The main role is taken by a small group of adolescents, among whom Gyuri Köves is far from being a leader. Rozi (Zsolt Dér) plays that role. Yet neither can Gyuri disappear among the adolescents, who regard the arrest as a joke. Gyuri does not have to participate in the general caper; a shade of boredom may appear in his eyes according to the psychology of the novel.

The location at Lórév has made the director come to an important decision. He has given up changing the view artificially, although earlier he considered including towers of the Shell Oil Refinery as an important part of depiction. Why?

"Earlier I regarded the site as some kind of world's end," says the director. "I planned several shots from the Customs House window with reference to that. We would have seen the towers of the oil refinery but I realised they had nothing to do with the story. I withdrew them from the electronic effects."

Undoubtedly, the policeman of József Szarvas in itself shows well what Lajos Koltai has perceived from the novel.

CAST OUT FROM THE NATION

27 January 2004. Shooting in a cattle track is the least spectacular matter. Lajos Koltai insists on absolute authenticity, the camera gets as near the deportees as if it were their companion. The Hungarian Railways have ensured the tracks at Szabadbattyán, otherwise used for servicing purposes, for shooting only today and tomorrow. Therefore, the director has to deal with a period happening much later compared to the scenes at Lórév. What can he do with a scene described by the script thus: "The people have become quiet. Many doze off with heads nodded forward. The boy muses." It will turn out at when the rushes are viewed.

A friendship develops between
Bandi and the boy

BELOW:

The relationship which will define
the end of the film is planned by
the director step by step

...from behind the camera

...and by checking the take on a monitor

29 January 2004. The railway station at Rákosrendező is Birkenau now. The selection officer, Sándor Zsótér, a blue-eyed theatre director, pushes Gyuri Köves towards those who temporarily stay alive. Something becomes obvious here among several hundred extras – Koltai has gone through a major change during the preparation for the film. Lajos Koltai, the beloved Sutyi, was always attentive, devoted and empathic during his career, in addition to his professional skills. In this respect he was like his master, György Illés, who was also able to execute his cinematographic ideas as if they had been the director's own. Now there is no 'Sutyi', but an extremely energetic director, who 'drives the people', who are otherwise inclined to sit down and wait for everything to fall in place for them. When I asked how conscious was the change, he answered with some bitterness: "The director has all the responsibility today. Everyone can ask me what to do, how to do it, and so on. I, however, can only ask the Lord what to do. I used to work on films when the assistant called the director out of the buffet when the scene was 'together'. That time is over. I must even make sure that what has been assigned for the day is done…"

"Because you have assured those who finance the film that *Fateless* will follow the wishes of Imre Kertész."

"Perhaps. Certainly it's best that I do not have any conflicts with Imre. I cannot spoil the novel. That's fixed. And the rest? You have to be not only hard but also cunning. I expect the maximum of everyone and there are some who have to be begged, others to be praised or reprimand, and so on. At the same time, I must make sure that I am fair with all."

30 January 2004. The shooting yesterday was nearly cancelled. Rumours spread that the film will be stopped. Lajos Koltai, however, insisted on going out on location, which required the highest number of extras. "It must be filmed," he said, and that is entirely natural of a director. The explanation, which he gave to only a few, is more astonishing. "Please understand that emotionally I want to be over with the selection at Birkenau."

The core crew returned to the studios from the Rákosrendező railway station to repeat the scene in Annamária's nursery.

31 January 2004. The first step in being an outcast from the nation is that your documents are taken away and you are kept in captivity. Gendarmes take over the herded Jews in the more than a century old police barracks, still working in Mosonyi Street behind the Eastern Railway Station. It is called Andrássy barracks in the novel. The boy still regards it as a senseless performance in which he does not know his role and he is most disturbed that his stepmother will not know in the evening where he is. When he goes through the first body search in his life he still feels like grinning. During the air-raid he realises the simplest truth: "Perhaps I began to understand a simple truth of the universe – I can be shot anywhere, any time". The sentence in the script is pronounced as voice over.

This summary presents it as a simple matter. In reality it is a two-day-long madness, moreover in twilight. Increasing numbers of new actors and actresses turn

Kollmann Senior
(Endre Harkányi)
and one of his sons,
Little Kollmann
(Márton Brezina)

Pictured together
for 'posterity' during
a stormy shooting

No tiny detail
is insignificant

Director, cameraman and gaffer, József Marton, check the authenticity of pictures

Meeting the Unlucky Man in the camp

up. They must prove to be 'in place' in short episodes. There are quite a few volunteers for the smallest roles, too.

Before dinner I have a few minutes to ask Lajos Koltai about the repeat which he viewed in the rushes. Why did they have to repeat the scene?

"I did not like the boy. However, the repeat was catastrophic. I don't think I can use any of the frames. The boy's head had became distorted as a result of the cold and in addition the dressers left his thermo-shirt underneath for the studio scene, too. The result was that the upper part of his body was different from before. To top it all, his voice was different so the sound immediately signalled that the hoarse voice cannot be used. But that is just the surface. In reality, it was another person who faced Annamária. The time between the two shootings made the boy a different person. It was frightening to see what had proved to be reality – it is impossible to return to the nursery after the Birkenau ramp. Chronological order doesn't make my work easier. Those who accuse me of that don't know what they're talking about, but it's the only way of shooting *Fateless*."

1 February 2004. Shooting continues in the twilight on Sunday. Four consecutive scenes have to be filmed in a two-kilometre-radius circle in the Újpest district of Budapest. In the story they actually precede what had happened in the Saturday shooting. They are sequences; the police are shepherding the herded Jews who are in lines of three. If there were not so many locations and not so many extras and onlookers it could be regarded as an easy job for a director. Of course, what Gyuri Köves says in the novel must also be reflected: "What I remember best about the long journey is the reaction of the passers-by watching our march. They had a kind of hurried, hesitant, almost furtive curiosity." Indeed, what lies ahead is fatally serious, but our main hero does not recognise that. A tram suddenly cuts the march in two and many take advantage of the unexpected moment to escape. It seems as if the accompanying policeman was encouraging Gyuri to flee, but he smiles, shrugs his shoulders and stays. So the sequence is not that easy. It is an important station; the boy can be reproached for the sin of a child's good faith.

There are many actors in the lines. Primarily those who appeared in the Customs House scene. The Unlucky Man, Bitter Face, The Expert or Seal Face are played by great actors like József Gyabronka, Miklós B. Székely, István Gőz and Béla Spindler.

This is a good opportunity to note Lajos Koltai's method of selecting actors. He had to cast one hundred and forty roles, which represented exactly a year's work. He compiled a list of all the Hungarian actors, inside and outside Hungary, with the most important data concerning whether he knew them or had worked with them before.

"I roped in everyone; there was no pre-selection," says Koltai. "I felt obliged to tell everyone what I thought of *Fateless*, how I wanted to shoot it, what style I wanted to work in, and so on. In the end I asked whether they would accept a role if on the day when I called them they had to say only one or two sentences, and even that may not be included in the film. 'Of course,' they said, without exception. 'That is why we are here.' And their word was as good as gold. They sometimes only played among the extras and many great faces were standing in the line without a complaint. It was like that with all the roles; it became clear after a long time that only he or she is the one to play it. It's true that I changed the actors many times until the 'moment of enlightenment'. They often criticised me, saying that I had told them the day before that they would play such and such a role, and then I appointed somebody else… I had two or three candidates for each role and I put off the decision until I was absolutely sure of the right person, and so it was with an aching heart that I turned down otherwise excellent actors."

3 February 2004. The crew moved to Paks because the brick dryer of the brickyard there most resembled that of the Budakalász brickyard in the novel. The shooting creates a stir in the small town. Everyone wants to watch, but only a few get near the location.[27]

By the end of the second day of shooting in Paks it could be said that one-third of the film is in the can, since the twentieth day of shooting planned for sixty days was today. Numbers of course do not mean a lot, still it is obvious that Lajos Koltai keeps to the original concept – he wants to depict the road leading towards the Holocaust and not only the Holocaust itself.

STANDSTILL

9 February 2004. The machinery has come to a halt today. Yesterday it was still churning properly at the military shooting range in Piliscsaba where the minister of culture, István Hiller, and the departing minister of finance, Csaba László, appeared. They could both see that the sets and costumes were 'consuming money'. Shooting has stopped. Journalists were given a really stupid explanation – the weather was too good or the strenuous work of the past week had exhausted the crew. So newspapers write: "Crew waiting for snow and fog – shooting at a standstill". I meet Lajos Koltai. "Please, announce that I have not said anything like that. By the way, I can be pleased about something; fortunately my concept is clearly apparent in the material filmed so far, and it is a very good feeling."

The scene of our conversation, the editing room, confirms that initial viewpoint. Takes we saw 'live' during shooting receive an original character now and become parts of a process. The process is the film itself. Of course it is too early to shout

---

[27] Mr Pál Wollner, an engineer of the nuclear power station, is, for example, among the few. He is an enthusiastic photographer and exhibited his photographs made during the shooting of *Fateless* in the Dunakömlőd Community Centre on 9 March. There are locals among the 250 extras wearing yellow stars. They are somewhat embarrassed in front of the camera, the reason being the small piece of yellow cloth. Pál Wollner, born in 1950, documents involuntarily that this story of our common past is not yet over.

A 'real' rest
between takes

Life is full of grotesque
moments: the film assistant
'preplays' the scene

The Arbeitskommando at work
unloading gravel

Rest at noon

"Hold your palm so, wondering what it's become like!"

'hurray' – film studios have always been noted for 'excellent' rushes and only when the film has been put together does it turn out that the whole was not good enough.

25 February 2004. Two weeks have gone by. The weather was like it usually is towards the end of winter, changeable, and this did not help a restart. More optimistic members of the production say that the new date will be 1 March. The more pessimistic ones wave their hand. "The boat is leaking, the holes must first be plugged." They make no secret of wanting to pass on this task to Lajos Koltai. More and more are snorting in the studios, too. "It was ridiculous to refer to the weather. The trouble is elsewhere." And so on. I do not want to immortalise what the critics say. The sad thing is that there are many who criticise.

3 March 2004. As a Hungarian saying puts it: "The older the child, the greater the problem." Every parent repeats it as the golden truth. What has reminded me of this? It was enough for me to see the deepening frowns on the 'parents' of *Fateless*. Public opinion, which more or less supported making the film until now, must be informed that filming is not happening today either. Lajos Koltai issues a statement, an unusual step for him. The director phones the Hungarian News Agency. He reads a few sentences and the employee of the official Hungarian news agency writes it down, then the noted organisation treats the statement as any other important news in international life: "The shooting of *Fateless* has halted due to temporary financial difficulties."

Such cool phrases are familiar these days. However, there is drama behind the words. Tonight Lajos Koltai spoke of a momentum in the drama.

"There is just a hole in place of my body, here in the middle. I am entirely emptied. All I am doing is dealing with financial matters, which I did not want."[28]
You say things like that in complete desperation or when your heart flounders in the captivity of zombies.

10 March 2004. The film must be made. Lajos Koltai tries the impossible, to be prepared cheerfully and freshly for a fight when his army in heavy armour has been climbing mountains day by day.

"Making a film is never positional warfare. It is rather like the Chinese long march. We are constantly on the move and the 'enemy', which is represented by the weather, badly concluded contracts, indisposed actors, careless members of the crew, missing props and thousands of other things, doesn't leave us alone for a moment. However, I'm used to that. That's my way of life. The frightening thing is that I don't spend most of my time in the company of the 'map' and my generals, namely the script and my actors, but am trying to pacify the heartland. I am searching eyes which look at me encouragingly. Of course, I'm complaining, but we can wonder why Hungarian film directors have to stand up for a fight with a rested

[28] *Tények* (Facts). TV 2, 3 March 2004

ABOVE: Roll call

BELOW: "The rows stagger as people lurch from exhaustion"

opponent when they have already had to win several hundred 'previous matches' beforehand."

24 April 2004. No, the film is not rolling today either but the situation is more hopeful than it was one and a half months ago. Imre Kertész appearing at the book festival provides the opportunity to note today's date. It would be good if many were able to remember what he said in an interview given on the occasion.

"We must give up, for example, self pity and the small-country complex."

Concerning the film adaptation of *Fateless*, after reiterating his support for Lajos Koltai, he said: "I have seen the rushes of the first hour, which convinced me that it is going to be a fine film after the great horror of the Christ film or *The Pianist*. It will be elevating and not distressing."[29]

Any opinion given in advance of a film still in the making is a sign of courage, since it can be later reproached. But why should not Imre Kertész be brave?

RESTART

10 May 2004. On 9 February I made the sad note that the machinery stopped that day. Now I am pleased to write that *Fateless* is being filmed again.

So events happened behind and not in front of the camera for two full months. What a struggle it was! Goodwill clashed with the facts – new producers do not seem to be prepared professionally to manage a super production. They swagger as if intoxicated, saying their production is solving a 'task'.

The Hungarian Cinema Foundation had to make a step and to its credit it made it. It established a company, Hungarian Cinema Ltd., which took the production of the film under its wing. We now meet names like Lajos Szakácsi, executive production manager, and Endre Sík, the co-producer. They are actually well-known in the profession. Szakácsi gained his experience in the former Mafilm and Sík worked in Hungarian Television to acquire the expertise necessary to get the machinery rolling.

When does a film crew work normally? It is actually a simple matter (though how difficult to do it): people have to be paid and artists must be allowed to feel artists, meaning creation must be a source of joy for them.

[29] Varsányi, Gyula (reporter): *Szoknunk kell Európában élni* (We must get used to living in Europe). *Népszabadság*, 24 April 2004. p. 12

János Bán, Judit Schell, Maciej Ciochki, Ágnes Olasz, Vilmos Kun, Piroska Molnár, Sándor Zsótér, Miklós Székely B.

An SS soldier (extra), Daniel Craig, a deportee (extra), András Kecskés M., Béla Paudits, Tibor Mertz, Sándor Kőműves, József Gyabronka

ABOVE: Baldy (Zoltán Bezerédi), a Stubendienst

BELOW: A master of life and death since he distributes food; now he is punishing

"DISMAL GRANDEUR"

19 May 2004. The 'roll' of the 32nd day of shooting is 'in the can' as of yesterday or rather last night because filming began at 6 p.m. and finished at dawn. Lajos Koltai's pleasure is the most notable thing these days. What pleasure; he jumps with joy. He is hyperactive. He announced a battle against the weather and at the moment is winning. During this period a shooting day only finished earlier than planned as a result of a downpour. The director appreciates every tiny success, whether it happens before the camera or behind. Such an almost strategic success is due to the fact that cameraman Gyula Pados seems to have psychologically accepted the unusual situation of his work being checked from take to take by the director, the undisputable master of the profession, whereas he himself was responsible for 'the pictures' in his films before.

The director's joy is contagious for his main character. Marcell Nagy, who lives in Gyuri Köves's skin, is at an age when facial features and especially the character change rapidly, which the film has put in another context as if 'the boy' has remained under 'civilian' conditions. At a relaxed moment, however, Koltai did not sigh accidentally: "Marci, how will I hand you back to your mother? She is expecting the old Marci, but you will remain Gyuri Köves for some time."

They are talking at the Zeitz camp, the second large exterior setting, which is part of the 'infringement of a taboo'. Imre Kertész made a note in the script: "The Holocaust, a pictorial, tangible and so to say 'realistic' depiction of the Nazi concentration camps clashes with a taboo based on a compromise. It is impossible to imagine the factory-like elimination of six million people and it must not be made imaginable. Their torment is indescribable and undepictable."

There is a single reason to infringe on the taboo in the case of *Fateless*. Since it follows the way of a soul, this way also leads through the death camps. Thus the location cannot be left out. The description of the camp in the novel was sufficient for Tibor Lázár to build the camp in the middle of fields near the village of Fót. What we see has emerged from the following few lines.

"A dusty flatland along the road. A square area torn from the landscape, which is bordered by barbed wire fencing and guard towers with spotlights in the four corners. Beyond the fence there are eight circus-size tents, which follow its line and looking at them from the front they make up a square."

Memory and the sight overturned Imre Kertész's sensation of time for a moment. When he was led into the just completed Block V, Gyuri Köves's 'dwelling' in the camp, the writer could only say: "I don't feel well now. I must leave."

The crew prepare an important scene at the site of the Duna Metal Works

The "ditch", a shelter for the deportees

An evening in the tent is a "single, complaining, plaintive groan"

Air-raid at the Arbeitskommando's plant

The crew are shooting in this location for two weeks. What does the genius loci do? The place affects those standing behind the camera. Most are professionals with a long experience. They have worked on Hungarian films for three decades on average. When Lajos Koltai looks at them their eyes show willingness and encouragement, including acknowledgement for the spot-on casting. Áron Dimény, in the role of Bandi Citrom, has been discovered in the far away Transylvania to teach the boy survival authentically. The psychological processes must be authentic. Koltai films the washing scene, which represents only a few sentences, with two cameras from four angles. He is satisfied: "One of the takes has what I wanted."

He is as much satisfied when the most horrible living situation in the camp, the real weight of time had to be filmed.

As Imre Kertész wrote, there had always been much time in the camp, and from one situation to the next you had to stand. Those who gave up, collapsed and they were punished badly. This life situation can only be depicted by scenes beyond words. To express the timeless time of collapse or remaining standing Koltai chose someone whose body really 'speaks'. Andrea Ladányi's desperate movement in the scene will be the telling sign. A miracle has presumably been born.

A question for today has remained. "How many miracles does a film need?"

"Many, very many," says Koltai and a troubled shadow passes over his face momentarily. The previous two months have not passed without a trace. Koltai's character as a director has become firm. That is not valuable in itself but is a typology. True, much can be seen in that. There are directors who *give orders*. They think about methods of execution all the time – how the actors should move, what the camera should do, when the crowd should get in the picture and what the take should be like to be similar to the loneliness of the surface of the moon. Then there are directors who *interpret*. They explain the situation, the antecedents and the consequences in an emphatic tone of voice to those standing before and behind the camera and underline what effect they must together achieve. Interpretation is a dangerous business – a director who regularly improvises will miss the target, and will surely be incorrect about what the desired character of an actor should be or what the significance is of a scene, a part of which was filmed two weeks before. It is not enough for the director to repeat commands for continuous *interpretation*. He must find an expression best characterising a situation in order to inspire his actors to achieve the best results. Lajos Koltai seems to be adding to the circle of interpreting directors. However, he does not use many gestures yet. It is noticeable that preparation for the shooting on the following day is a lonely operation for him. Alone he must find the secret, which he shares with the others the next day.

20 May 2004. Did the enforced halt wear down the crew? No, only one key person left as a result. Hungarian crew members were less nervous than expected. The majority of important participants restarted work with a kind of nostalgia – they have experienced large productions and remember what it means to make a 'super film' in that sense.

Simon Kaye, the Oscar-winning British sound engineer, waited. He did so out of friendship – faithfulness does not pay in a 'business sense'. Kaye is a real key player – the bulk of the sound for *Fateless* will not be recorded in the studio but on location. Two fundamental conditions must be ensured in order to use so-called direct sound: absolute silence when the film is rolling and the actors must not make a mistake. Post-dubbing can correct a lot, although the unrepeatable atmosphere of the take is lost. Since the latter is important, every sound must be 'in place' in the case of direct sound. Although Simon grumbles a little at each take, he is satisfied with the silence during shooting.

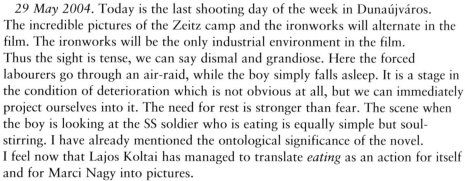

"In Italy, there is always some chatting behind the camera," he says. "In Hungary everything could be solved so far. We have found the best position for my microphone assistant."

The sound recording is conducted in a traditional way entirely, without microwave technique. Surely, the sound of *Fateless* will not be coming from a barrel. Does it not disturb Simon that he does not speak Hungarian? No. The director is responsible for the content of the modulation, it is his responsibility if the actor is false.

29 May 2004. Today is the last shooting day of the week in Dunaújváros. The incredible pictures of the Zeitz camp and the ironworks will alternate in the film. The ironworks will be the only industrial environment in the film. Thus the sight is tense, we can say dismal and grandiose. Here the forced labourers go through an air-raid, while the boy simply falls asleep. It is a stage in the condition of deterioration which is not obvious at all, but we can immediately project ourselves into it. The need for rest is stronger than fear. The scene when the boy is looking at the SS soldier who is eating is equally simple but soul-stirring. I have already mentioned the ontological significance of the novel. I feel now that Lajos Koltai has managed to translate *eating* as an action for itself and for Marci Nagy into pictures.

Today the boy has to collapse under the weight of a cement sack. The scene itself is not narrative. The director is not interested where the cement is taken from or to.

The boy's exhaustion overcomes fear

Last instructions before a difficult take

Hunger at midday

"Let's try to endure"

He is concentrating only on the process of sacking with special respect to the adolescent child. The boy has to lift real weight. No compromise.

"I don't want to have sacks filled with polystyrene," says the director. "I cannot ask the children to act as if they had a huge weight on their backs. But at the same time I do not want them to crumble under the weight. So something suitable must be found."

Thus fifteen kilos seemed to be bearable during the whole day of shooting. That corresponds to the description in the novel, since Imre Kertész is also talking about reduced sacks.

BUCHENWALD

3 June 2004. Lajos Koltai filmed the scenes in the Rehmsdorf hospital yesterday and today. It is an ontological sequence again. Marci Nagy is acting out *starvation*. He is more precisely in a situation when the fear of starvation wins over a larger fear, death. But to make the phenomenon more complex, the highest instance of mercy appears in the same scene in the person of a deportee distributing food.

Koltai proceeds from take to take in the dust and mist of the barrack. This scene could have been shot earlier if the heating had been turned on. Now it should be cooled but of course that cannot be done. There is nothing else to do but to wipe the sweat off the foreheads and drink a couple of litres of mineral water. The extras can at least lie on the beds. I can even see someone who has fallen asleep amidst the hustle. Not so Béla Paudits, the bony actor who entertains his audience with stories during the breaks. Nor does he mind how much he will be in the film. He is here and that means he was needed.

4 June 2004. The audience will have a view of the camp from today's shooting. The 'slogan' of Buchenwald, JEDEM DAS SEINE – "Everyone His Own". The pictures, however, will not only inspire the viewer to contemplate. The arrival of the ill and dying is a shocking sight. Gyuri Köves is somewhere among the twisted bodies. When the dying are watered we catch sight of him. Lajos Koltai is extremely conscious about showing the main hero either by a close-up or as the member of the community whose fate interlocks with that of the others.

"In the film fates pass by and one from among them suddenly becomes more important. But even he who stands further in the line has a fate. No one has a fixed place actually. At a given moment the person standing in the back becomes important and his fate will be a strong sign on the main hero's way of the cross."

In this concept the size of frames is also significant. It enables many to fill in the space behind the boy, especially faces which bear their own fate. I ask whether it was possible for the film not to close off the fate of those who stand further away, perhaps in order to make it roll more rapidly. Lajos Koltai answers quietly but with intent.

"I cannot do it. What support has the boy in this world? A familiar face. If he still sees it the following day, he is reassured and finds something to hang on to. If he does not see it he also becomes aware that a new station follows. He remains increasingly alone and that weakens not only his body but also his existence."

This 'thesis' is best supported by Bandi Citrom's fate. He is no longer present at Buchenwald. His fate will be clear at the end of the film, at an emphatic place in line with the script.

The weather is very important in today's scene. An urban dweller would say that the weather is bad, with stormy wind and rain. Here, however it is fortunate. The crew are not sitting idly they are shooting, even when we would think it is impossible. Everyone puts on long raincoats and the reality is supplemented with the artificial elements of the weather which not only recall winter but make the dark condition of existence tangible, showing that the boy has arrived at a new station. The carrot soup cauldrons play an important role in today's takes. Hunger dominates memory and the boy no longer remembers his family but only the soup they had together in the past.

5 June 2004. After the bath, where the showerheads let out water this time, there is one of the most shocking scenes of the film. The sight of the naked dead reduced to bones is marked by a single sentence in Kertész's script: "From the perspective of a hanging head we see a few prisoners pulling a flat trailer piled with dead bodies." Here, words are replaced by pictures which, however, must not be similar to the familiar documentary photographs. Nevertheless, they have to be authentic. Koltai uses a special technique for the special moment, although it

Grapple over an exchanged bowl of soup between the Finn (András Kecskés M.) and the boy

is no longer interesting when looking at the ready shot. The professional question of 'how' will be entirely replaced by the 'what has it become' controllable by everyone.

7 June 2004. The Buchenwald camp has been liberated from Saturday to Monday, that is today. There is no flag waving or big celebration. Although there will be a few hospital scenes with the boy before today's takes, an essential part of *Fateless*, that liberation takes place, is done. Yet as in history, liberation has not resolved the issue of the Holocaust. It has revealed it to the world.

The story of returning home begins and we must first go through the choice of going home. In his own life, Marci Nagy has travelled a lot in the world with his parents, despite his young age, so he knows what going home means. He is able to make us feel that the scene is about nothing else but the notion of *arrival home*.

8 June 2004. The last day in the Buchenwald camp. An extra tells me that his mood has completely changed since the camp was liberated. Lajos Koltai is expecting guests today. He would like to show the location to his noted colleagues. They arrive – Miklós Jancsó, István Szabó, Ferenc Grunwalsky, Tamás Tolmár, the director of Mafilm and his team, the supervisory board of the Hungarian Cinema Foundation. István Lénárt, who introduced Lajos Koltai to Hungarian Television, thought it important to appear dressed with his usual elegance. These artists and professionals still know what solidarity means. I also have a role in showing the guests around. I know the locations and the scenes filmed by heart. The shooting

The overseer, soldier Todt, retaliates for the expensive material being ruined

range at Piliscsaba affects everybody, but no one suggests that it should be maintained as a 'tourist sight'. The set will have the same destiny as the script; it will disappear. Perhaps the former more so, since the script may continue to exist in book form, but the set will become waste wood to be fired.

The guests do not wait for the last take to be shot at twilight at the end of a long day. It will be a shot of the working chimney of the crematorium.

ON THE WAY HOME

10 June 2004. Filming continues in the studio today. We have been here once before, the Fleischmanns' flat. I do not have to look it up in my notes. Edit Nagy the ever-reliable production co-ordinator, immediately says: "Wednesday, 21 January." That was nearly five months ago. According to Lajos Koltai's concept, the scene between the returning Gyuri Köves and the old people can only be filmed now. The boy not only has to understand what the difference is in Gyuri between the two scenes, he also had to go through it. It is anyway surprising that the set is still intact. The director explains what happened.

"I was first told that to keep it was impossible. Production wanted me to shoot the end of the film while we were there. 'You've gone off your mind,' I said. 'It's impossible professionally.' They kept alarming me saying that the set was going to be dismantled. So I answered, never mind, you can rebuild it. There was a big disagreement. Unfortunately, even some of those very close to me in the crew supported the production side."

A sip of water before the next take

The boy looks at the soldier
"baffled, humbly and expectantly"

The take will be at night but the extras must know by then what their role is in the story

The make-up must be such that the wounds show the condition of the three prisoners

The end of a hopeless attempt to escape

Today, in addition to the scene where Ádám Rajhona and György Barkó add a bit of irony, which protects the end of the film from any sentimentalism due to natural sympathy, Lajos Koltai also films a special image, a soup-tureen – the single flash-back in the film, which flashes in the boy's mind when he sees the carrot soup cauldrons on arrival at Buchenwald.

The script included several flash-backs but, like some of the voice overs, started to become alien to the filmed material. For example, in the Rehmsdorf barrack the boy remembers how the doctor arrived at their house in the past. When the carefully taken frame of the soup-tureen is 'canned', Koltai explains why he cannot use the flash-backs.

"A station of the boy's way of the cross is that he doesn't remember. It's a tragic station since everybody hangs on to his memories to the last ditch. However, the boy doesn't recall anything other than what hunger brings up. Therefore, the faces of the father, stepmother or Annamária do not appear from the mist of the past, as they say. The only thing he remembers is the soup-tureen, though it was not included in the script."

12 June 2004. Today is Saturday and the closure of Lőrinc pap Square is ensured. So the last take of the film must be shot today, which according to the script must be "as if it was covered by some golden light, some kind of silent irreality we have already seen in the camp."[30] The light, which is invisible yet still making objects visible, must be similar to what Lajos Koltai has already produced in the Zeitz camp, in a long shot, involving no artificial lighting. In order to do that, you must thoroughly know nature, which is able to evoke a similar spectacle both in the city and the country. The camera films the scene in golden twilight at the end of a sunny day. Koltai is confident that he has managed to create the atmosphere of "silent irreality" in the urban scene. It required the scene to be taken now since the essence is that we return to where the film started.

"Among others things, I mean by irrationality or 'silent irreality' that the boy is standing in the same square where the story began. Some people said that we should have filmed this during the first weekend when the beginning takes of the film were shot. I was amazed at such insensitivity. I thought, 'Surely they are not talking to me!' I rejected the idea right away but a thorn remained in me. Therefore, I may not have immediately accepted some good ideas and needed some time while I thought them over, whether they really serve the film or they again want to send me up the garden path."

Also today a scene follows which was included in the script during shooting with the agreement of both the writer and director. By combining two episodes Gyuri Köves pronounces the hardest statement of the novel amidst the constant rattle of a tram. After shooting finishes at dawn, the director summarises the result of the long ride on the tram.

[30] This quotation reveals the perfect harmony between the writer working with concepts and the director painting with light.

Bandi Citrom and Big Kollman (Péter Fancsikai) will help the boy get up from the mud

Being lonely in front of the hospital tent

ABOVE: A lorry takes the sick to the Rehmsdorf "hospital"

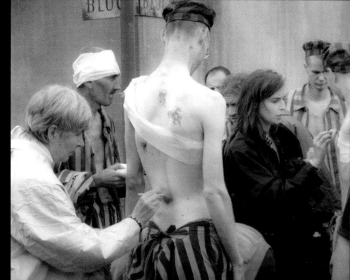

Maddening hunger

The director in the hospital barrack in Rehmsdorf

Marci rests there

Marci is obsessed with taking photographs; next to his mother, Éva

"There is no doubt that Gyuri Köves had to be made to say that the only feeling he has after his arrival home is hatred. But he says it without being indignant or moved, without passion or anger, which is the result of him not finding any component of his past in its place."

14 June 2004. The Hungarian Railways allowed the area of the Istvántelek Carriage Repairs to be used as the scene of the ruined railway station. It is an excellent location, hardly twenty minutes away from the studios.
Lajos Koltai must create the detachment of the scene shot two day before here, while remaining with the internal unity of the experience.
The boy and the former, successful child actor, Csaba Gieler, who created a fate from the role of the interpreter, discuss the ontology of *survival* almost casually while walking around the ruined station. Gieler must make the viewers see what the humane consequence of survival can be. "He who has died once cannot be angry any more."

15 June 2004. The first day of shooting was exactly half a year ago. There is no time to celebrate this silent 'anniversary'. Two episodes of home coming have to be filmed at the Western Railway Station. One is movingly emotional – women are standing with photographs as people arrive home. The questions are always the same. "Have you seen him? Do you know anything about him?" We must, however, remember the discussion between Imre Kertész and the director regarding the basic atmosphere of the film: "emotional but not melodramatic". And Lajos Koltai is careful that the episode which may well make people weep would not become sentimental. It is also a question of length. He does not utilise all the possibilities of the scene but interrupts it with questions to the boy by a strange character from the novel who would like to resolve the issue of gas chambers according to the rules of formal logic. "Did gas chambers actually exist?" And, as if satisfied, he summarises the answer. "You, personally did not ascertain their existence with your own eyes." There is no logical response to the question – a survivor cannot give an account of gas chambers.

16 June 2004. According to the novel Bandi Citrom lived in Nefelejcs Street, in the Budapest district of Ezsébetváros. The location is near there, at 37 Munkácsy Mihály Street, Terézváros. In the corridor of the 19th century tenement block, dating from the time when Budapest turned into a metropolis, the boy hurries to find first the person to whom he owed most in Zeitz – with *hope* that he had survived 'the lot'. Bandi's fate in the book is obvious from the dialogue between mother and daughter. Lajos Koltai leaves some uncertainty in the text but the actress, Ági Olasz's eyes depict Bandi Citrom's fate tragically. It is a perfect example of the basic difference between how literature and film express the same content.
Koltai does not contemplate – he sets the composition and lighting, instructs the actors and he does all that without tiredness until he, alone, thinks that the scene is ready for editing. He does not make it a secret that the film will get its final form in

the editing room, whereby the fine interplay of motifs and emphasis making up the takes will turn into what is art – the finished film.

17 June 2004. The film depicts the impossibility of home coming in a direct and indirect sense on the last shooting day in Hungary – directly in that the Köves flat is occupied by unknown people who have been bombed out. The situation is told by two short takes – from out to in and in to out. Here it is not a mechanical matter which is involved, but the two aspects represent two different viewpoints. Correction follows correction – the picture size is not for such close-ups. In a certain sense it prevents the camera from getting too close to the character's face, thus making the film more objective, like the concept behind the novel. Although Koltai makes it obvious that Gyuri Köves's viewpoint is most important for him, he still keeps his own viewpoint.

The indirect depiction of the impossibility of home coming is interesting – the rhyming pair to the staircase scene with Annamária is taken. Imre Kertész and Lajos Koltai also regarded closing this line as important. Nevertheless, it is not overemphasised, since Annamária has lost the emotional touch the boy must have felt at the first meeting on the staircase. However, she is a significant character at the end of the film. She asks: "What do you look like?" Thinking he would look better, the boy takes off his cap, which makes the contrast with the first staircase meeting more shocking. Then Annamária puts the question, which in Imre Kertész's experience is the most stupid concerning the Holocaust: "Was it very … horrible?" The reply is astounding. "No." Then the boy smiles.

The set is the same as it was at the beginning of the film. The only difference is that then the boy was coming up the stairs but now it is the girl with the bread bag, which was in the boy's hand before. The roles have changed, that is all. It is not a special idea, since the scene tells us that the boy is leaving the house for ever, he is going away. However, the dialogue ends again with a 'story' – the boy quotes the interpreter. "I have already died once… So I can no longer be angry."

Lajos Koltai seems to be pleased to talk about the film with anybody, anywhere. Today, for example, a group of people led by the former minister of finance called by. The ministry may act as sponsors. The director told them what had to be done that day and how that fitted into the whole. He did not show how much lay people's questions exasperated him. He has learnt that that is also part of the profession and it being so he must take it seriously. It means his lunchtime will be shorter than for the others.

István Szabó is also present. He does not ask anything but hands over a bottle of champagne. "Well, we are over this one, too," he says embracing Lajos who is moved by the gesture. The long march is nearing its end.

The boy at the Buchenwald station for the second time

Béla Paudits and Marci relax between two takes

The Protesting Man (Béla Paudits) resists to his last breath

For whom the road has ended

The director checks the spectacle from all angles

Avant de mourir: "The cart is pushed by both hands. The Boy has no doubt where he is going"

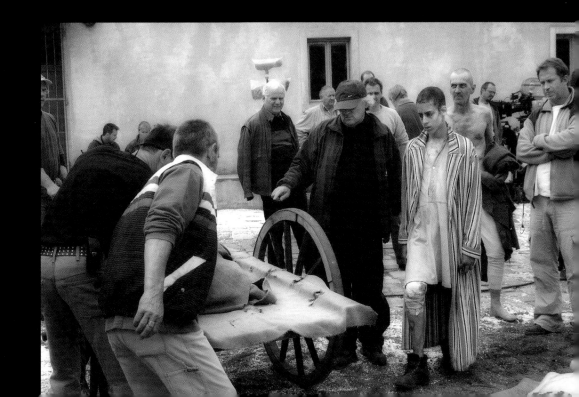

"He is watching everything from far away, and yet as someone who sees the colours of the Earth for the last time"

The take of the cart scene

Simon's expression betrays that it is not only the clarity of sound which is important in this scene

In the grave pit

He looks at the shower nozzle of the bath

The water
streams down ▶

Marci naturally gets the most attention
before takes...

He likes being liked by everyone

The miracle: the boy is taken to hospital

The world from the perspective of the hanging head

The boy in the hospital bed

The life-saving operation (cut from the film)

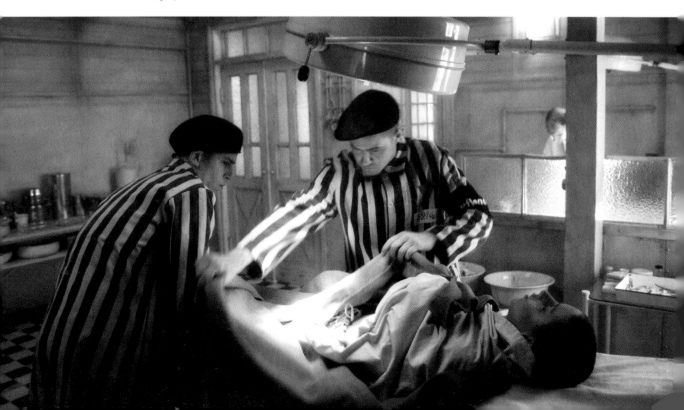

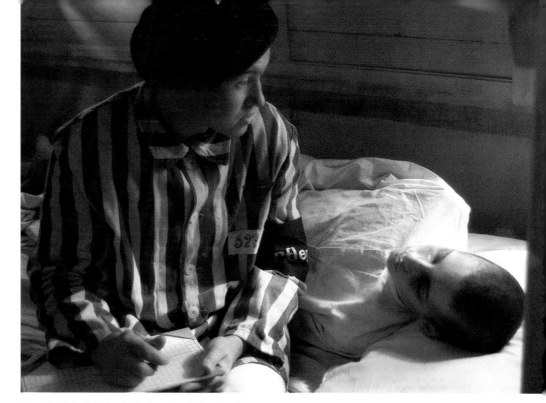

Pjetyka (Maciej Ciochki) gives back the boy's name

The Hungarian patient (Ferenc Horváth)

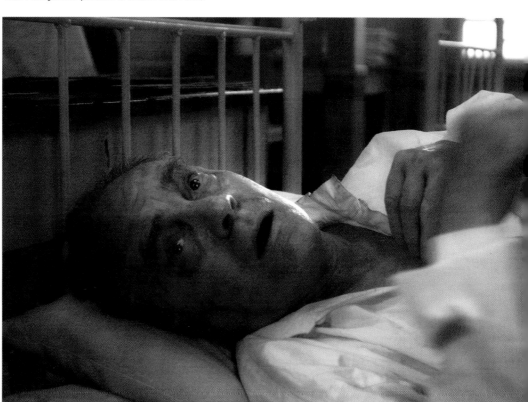

IN GERMANY

22 June 2004. We are at the ruins of a paper mill just outside Merseburg. Those who know about Hungarian history will remember that the knights of Henry I, the Fowler, inflicted a defeat on the raiding Hungarians putting them to flight at the battle field of Merseburg in 933 – feigning on this occasion was not successful. That mournful event hardly shadows the mood. Lajos Koltai intends to stay here for only one day. There is no time to contemplate the past, not even on the past of filming. The crew has an important day ahead. It is the first day of shooting in Germany. It means that the production of *Fateless* is taking place in a normal way. András Hámori, 'the replacement producer' has managed to sort things out with his love for the cause and his international experience. The German co-operation, which at one point was doubtful, is proceeding according to plan. Moreover, the staff of EuroArts Medien AG., the partner company from Berlin, seem to have prepared thoroughly. Most amazingly, the German crew immediately get into the mood which has characterised shooting so far. Without doubt, 'dismal grandeur' also affects them.

According to Imre Kertész's script, scene five of the third part has to be filmed today. (It is the 137th in Lajos Koltai's script.) At the location the sky looms beyond the crooked ruins of the paper mill. Buda Gulyás, also working as a cameraman here, knows how, when the film is completed, there will be the distant ruins of Dresden in the background. This addition is necessary. We must see what Gábor Máté is talking about. Máté turns the supporting role of 'Uncle Miklós' into a real performance. He gives a speech here about Dresden to the deportees who are on their way home. He tries to make the survivors accept that the Germans, living now in rat holes, have got what they deserved. A dangerous view.

"This will turn into resentment," says Imre Kertész, "which is the breeding ground for dictatorship." It is the basis of a historical approach which perceives human history as the uninterrupted process of give and get. The scene shows that there are some who agree with Uncle Miklós, the good organiser, and there are some who keep quiet. The boy in this scene stands before one of the most difficult trials – he must give weight to the scene merely with the look in his eyes and without any action.

The director is in his element. Constant duties seem to perk him up and perhaps the light at the end of the tunnel can already be seen. Filming continues smoothly. When the day ends they make their way to the headquarters in Erfurt. However, a small group do not return there directly: Zeitz is situated between Merseburg and the centre of county Thüringia. Tibor Lázár, the scenery designer, has been here before, although it was in winter. He does not encourage the director promising a memorable spectacle. Truly, the residents of Zeitz did not wish to remember the camp connected to Buchenwald, from where the deportees were marched out daily to slave labour in the near-by factory. Today the factories in the neighbourhood are modern, in no way recalling Braunkohle-Benzin-Aktiengesellschaft, which in the

Marci makes
his way
from the
changing
room upstairs

Lajos Koltai
checks the set
from behind
the camera

The sweet chaos of liberation
on the neglected Appellplatz

LEFT TO RIGHT:

Happily wearing the strange Polish officer's cap

Marci as a mature 'civilian' at the same place

Gyula Pados, however, is thinking even now; getting tuned on the next task

An American jeep among the loitering camp residents

The boy in front of the mirror again

"I remember another face from the past"

The director and Marci, the latter touched on receiving Koltai's 'family present'

The American sergeant (Daniel Craig) advises the boy to stay in the Western zone

The director
explains what is
at stake with
the decision

The lorry is ready to depart with those returning home; the sergeant in a last attempt to make the boy stay

Daniel Craig and the parasol

novel was 'visited' by aeroplanes several times. One or another still produces oil products.

We also go to Rehmsdorf, the location of the Zeitz camp hospital. We look up the house at 1 Beethoven Street. The gate is open but unfortunately we learn from the neighbours that Mr Lothar Czossek and his wife are on holiday, so we do not meet the local resident who collected and publicised the documents of the Zeitz camp and the Rehmsdorf hospital. However, we find a modest plaque by the small station. It condemns the Nazi genocide in general, delicately avoiding concrete matters connected to the place.

The station is exactly as István Hajdú had described it. Time does not seem to have changed it. Hajdú must also certainly be remembered. Koltai had known the former employee of the film studios, but only after *Fateless* had been in the limelight did he disclose that he had been one of the six-eight adolescents who had been on the Auschwitz–Buchenwald–Zeitz death march with the future writer, moreover that he had been held captive in the same barrack. He was taken back to Buchenwald in February 1945 where he lost a leg due to a bombing raid. Hajdú had managed to survive, thanks to some inexplicable reason, and had been able to return home, but he had deeply buried what he had gone through as an adolescent, just like many others who shared that fate. However, he also opened up.

Our car makes a semicircle on a bumpy side-road. Lajos Koltai suddenly becomes excited but we also see that this small part of the Thüringian landscape looks exactly like the area near Fót, where the set of the Zeitz camp was constructed. It is not difficult to mentally project *that* Zeitz camp into this place. The camp suddenly becomes realistic here for a few minutes, as we all sink into silence.

24 June 2004. The SS hospital ward and operating theatre have been constructed in an empty warehouse near Arnstadt, where the young Bach was a choir-master at the local church. The original was in Buchenwald where Gyuri Köves found a frightening sentence going through his mind in the last stage of his deterioration.

"And in spite of any other consideration, rational thought, feeling of resignation or of common sense, I still couldn't mistake the furtive words of some kind of quiet desire rising within myself, as if embarrassed because of their senselessness, but yet consistently stubborn in their persistence: I would so much like to live a little longer in this beautiful concentration camp."

Lajos Koltai has discovered the boy in Marcell Nagy. The young Nagy has been able to interpret even such complex thoughts, as we saw on several occasions during shootings in Hungary.

Marcell Nagy, the impersonator of Gyuri Köves, lives in the centre of Budapest and attends a Calvinist school. His parents have been keen on sport, moreover in running the Marathon and in pentathlon, the two most demanding fields. Marcell has also proved rather talented in two parts of the latter, swimming and running. Yet, those who are looking for something 'extraordinary' in the child will be disappointed. At the same time, it is obvious that he is more developed psychologically, more sensitive and more mature than his peers. He is strikingly disciplined, a feature he certainly required given such a long and demanding film.

Before the take the director and the set designer, Tibor Lázár,
suddenly have urgent business in opposite directions

Deportees returning home, the Interpreter (Csaba Geiler), Uncle Miklós (Gábor Máté)
and the boy are resting by the ruins of Dresden

Either his father or mother was present during the shootings, which gave some comfort to Lajos Koltai, since he did not have to worry about the child being over-pampered. When not appearing in a scene, he was under parental supervision. At the same time, the director took the opportunity of trying to fit into Marcell's small and compact family as, for example, an uncle; and he succeeded. He got to very much like Marcell, who in return trusted him, a trait usually only bestowed on closed family members. At the end of the filming Marci will even 'get a family present' from the director as a surprise.

When it was necessary, the extremely modest Marcell, who is more vivid than anyone, five to ten times repeated a word, whose intonation the director described, explaining its meaning with simple words but never showing how to do it. However, today he has to solve a simple but vitally important scene: he has to look into a mirror and state: "All in all I considered myself fit, aside from a few strangenesses, and the like." Imre Kertész's script exactly describes the fact of survival and helps it with a voice over, but it is still 'short' compared to the detailed description in the novel. During the preparation for the scene it can be clearly seen how many factors are required to be present at the same time to 'interpret' it authentically. Everything, from the objects, like the mirror itself, to lighting, from the angle to the adjustment of the camera's technical parameters, contributed to the fact that Marcell Nagy, a Budapest pupil, who would slide down the banister from his dressing room upstairs to the level of the studio, would become Gyuri Köves at the moment of a miracle – he had not seen his own face for months. Now he recoils, for as much time as is required for the viewer to recall the child seen at the beginning of the film, when he said farewell to his father, and to quickly contemplate the process of deterioration divided into stations.

Gyuri Köves's amazement at his long unseen face in the mirror is a poetically dense moment and is like a summary. This picture, without any words, could be the symbol of a fate 'accidentally' tipped off its normal course. At the end of the day Lajos Koltai quietly remarks: "It's worth making a film for such moments."

But work has not finished yet. As usual, Koltai does not get involved in the evening relaxation of the crew. However, no one blames him – they know this is the time when he makes the notes he conjures from his pocket before each take the following day. Although he knows the score by heart, he has learnt that every day on location a director must appear in a perfect condition, both intellectually and physically. He is allowed to be helped (with notes) and a long sleep is always recommended (although it is not always possible).

26 June 2004. We have come this far. According to the unwritten rules of shooting, the crew photograph is made after the last clapper board. It includes many people (even I was asked to join in). The almost compulsory tear drop was in most people's eyes. Marcell Nagy sobbed a bit as a result of the digital camera he received as a 'family present'. His father remarked: "Marci has never been so happy with a present."

Most people became emotional, since a sort of painful nostalgia for old time Hungarian film making permeated the shooting of *Fateless*, for the era when work

FACING PAGE:
The boy with
a piece of bread

On the way home through the streets of a small German town

The washroom in Erfurt before the take

The former SS soldier (Máté Haumann) does not take his shirt off

Gaffer József Marton

Last instructions

ABOVE: The scene with the Interpreter (Csaba Gieler) and the boy at the ruined railway station fell victim to cutting

BELOW: Uncle Miklós the organiser; the Communists will be able to rely on him

ABOVE: Now the cattle trucks are taking the deportees home

BELOW: Women at the railway station in Bratislava

The questioning man (Miklós Molnár) asks: "Did you see the gas chambers?"

was to schedule and professional. That essentially characterised the 1960s and 1970s, when respected great film makers and up-coming youngsters were present and financial security still prevailed. The gaffer, József Marton says: "I used to work on films of this volume once a year. Of course, it was not the size that mattered but the big task, which raised the self-esteem of professionals."

The temporary studio in Arnstadt worked well – the three days shot here will easily connect to the takes in Hungary. Buda Gulyás was the cameraman replacing Gyula Pados.[31] He was good as the right hand of the director and he captured the basic atmosphere of the film without any difficulty.

Lajos Koltai had to film economically, and not only because of the German crew and the management of EuroArts who paid a visit to Erfurt. Efficiency is not for its own sake but 'preparation for editing'. In filming Koltai seemed to be following Bergman, who says that editing takes place in the camera and only the instructions of the camera must be followed in the editing room.

"During shooting I was always making film which prepared for the next step, because of lack of time, too," says Koltai. "That is why it will be easy to edit. Shooting is no entertainment. Yes, we are finishing one phase of the film. But a new one, editing, will start on Monday. That's usually the most frightening part because it's there that the director can realise he's 'forgotten' to film the most

[31] The reason why Gyula Pados could not finish the film was due to the suspension. The film *Stop Mummy Theresa!* could no longer wait for him, and he did not want to let down his director friend, Péter Bergendy. Pados said in an interview that it was difficult for him to get into *Mummy Teresia*. As therapy: "Bergendy and I watched comedy films and listened to entertaining music for two days so that after the Holocaust on Friday I could film young people dancing in the bar New Orleans on Monday." Kati Gőzsy (reporter): *Index*. 19 July 2004

The nameplate of Bandi Citrom's family in a "dark, musty gateway" in Nefelejcs Street

The fate of the best friend can be seen in the eyes of Bandi's sister (Ági Olasz) and his mother (Mari Csomós)

A stranger's face (Anikó Gruiz) at the door of the Köves flat

"As if nothing had changed"; the neighbours plan the boy's future

important viewpoint or another atmosphere should have been given to a scene. But there's no mercy – only what we have shot can be put in the film. However, I'm alright. I hope we've shot everything we had to. Moreover, I could make montages from the filmed material, but it wouldn't make sense since they would surely not fit in."

Self-confidence is based on facts in the present case. The break in filming had some 'use' since it was possible to begin editing, the concept of montage could be clarified and it also allowed time before a trip to Erfurt, in secret as was befitting, to show the writer the incomplete, two hour long material without dialogue and with temporary music. Imre Kertész knew exactly what the characters were saying because of the situations and he was practically delighted with the barely half-ready film. On the one hand, he praised its authenticity including the extras' faces. On the other, he captured the distance, namely the consistent constraint, avoiding melodramatic calculation for effect. He approved of the dialogues becoming shorter. "Well, we can see what needs to be said," as Koltai interpreted the writer's

The one
who has changed

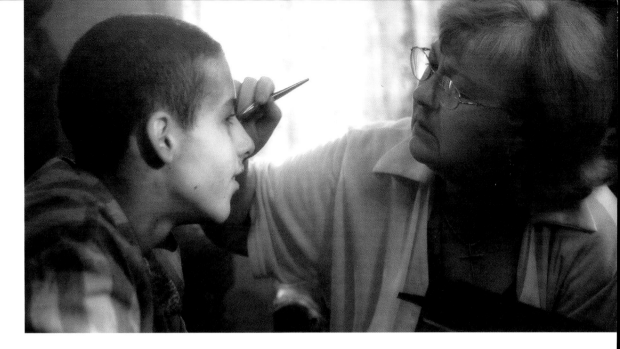

The make-up artist carefully makes
the external signs of change tangible

Aunt Fleischmann (Kati Lázár)

203

Meeting Annamária in the stairway. "Was it horrible?"

response. For Kertész the screening resonated for a long time. He kept returning to what he had felt at the meeting Zsuzsa Radnóti had arranged for the 'inner circle'. In the end he called Koltai aside and offered his considered opinion.

"I have already died once"

"I did not believe that anybody would be able to translate the novel into a film. But I think you have succeeded."

IS THE FILM BEING MADE NOW?

Only the first phase of the 'long march' had finished with the last shooting day. The second, perhaps less spectacular but equally important second stage immediately began. That stage is usually simply called post-production, although those specialising in the art of cinema say that a film is in the editing state, since the intimate activity in the editing room gives a film the form which the viewer will see. It also presents the impossibility of writing about what was conducted in the case of *Fateless* all summer, although Lajos Koltai had taken advantage of the enforced stoppage to experiment with the style of editing. Even Koltai's fracture of the shoulder bone does not affect the procedure. It was literally nailed together. It hurt him a lot. Nevertheless, everyone said: "How lucky that it has happened now."

When editing the director usually shows the 'film still requiring further work' to only those from whom he expects new ideas or confirmation, or who have further tasks in post-production. For example, the composer, Ennio Morricone, born in Rome on 10 November 1928, is such a person. Koltai met him when he was

The director interprets the boy's great end-of-film monologue again
and again in the square which also played a role in Lajos Koltai's life

The miracle, however, can only be born before the camera

filming in Italy. The composer became fond of the Hungarian cameraman, who, as he said, "served the music to soar with suitable pictures", since Morricone's music is no effect-seeking scraping but real soaring. Now the maestro can afford to take on a job he likes. Therefore, even back in 2002 he asked the future director what his intention was concerning the book, which had become a great success in Italy, too. He was quiet for hours then sat down by the piano and played a few bars from the piece he had in the meantime composed. Thus Koltai could come up with the sensation that Ennio Morricone was going to compose the music, unless he withdraws after seeing the film. Morricone viewed the film in Rome in the director's presence. The end result was to organise recording in Hungary as soon as possible because the music was ready in his head.

It was organised and recording began in the noted Studio 22 of Hungarian Radio on 4 October 2004. To characterise the music let me say that the participants included Lisa Gerrard, a Australian singer with a wonderful voice, Szakály Ágnes, a dulcimer artist from Budapest, and Ulrich Herkenhoff, a pan-pipe player from Berlin. Then came less spectacular ordinary days. These also left their imprint on the film, just like the special days, which became brighter as the shooting receded into the past.

The first Hungarian digital negative corresponding to the conceived images was ready in London. How it was made is impossible to describe in a few lines, even for

"To gather my strength I've stopped at the square for a minute"

A spectacular moment of post-production – recording
the music; the singer from Australia (Lisa Gerrard),
the composer from Italy (Ennio Morricone)

The Maestro

A thank you for the music

professionals, though naturally for the viewer what matters will be the particular end result. Finally, it was in Berlin where the film received its sound, which makes the experience of *Fateless* one for our ears, too. Simon Kaye ensured the clarity of the dialogues, the life-like sound and the atmosphere, involving nerve-wrecking work which only our hearing can detect. Obviously, perfect film sound is not limited by any frame, unlike with the picture. It fills the space and therefore the adjustment of sound to picture is a real art, which necessarily involves pure directorial intention.

How much work! How many enthusiastic participants! Not to mention those important people who did their best for the film without being members of the crew. However, below we include the list of visible crew members without an attempt at entirety. We know that some of the audience is already restless in the cinema at that moment. Reading it here they may appreciate that it was they whose eyes looking into those of Lajos Koltai most often felt the trust without which the film could not have been made.

THE FILM MAKERS AND THE CAST

Directed by Lajos Koltai
Director of photography:
Gyula Pados H.S.C.
Screenplay by Imre Kertész
Produced by András Hámori
Editor: Hajnal Sellő H.S.E.
Sound: Simon Kaye AMPS, CAS
Costumes: Szakács Györgyi
Production designer: Lázár Tibor
Music by Ennio Morricone
Associate producers:
Endre Sík (Budapest),
Jonathan Haren (London),
Tibor Krsko (Budapest),
Michael Reuter (Berlin)
Cooproduction partners:
Ildiko Kemeny (London), Jonathan
Olsberg (Berlin), Péter Barbalics
(Budapest)
Supervising Producer:
Lajos Szakácsi
Executive Producers: László Vincze,
Bernd Hellthaler, Robert Buckler

CHARACTERS IN ORDER
OF APPEARANCE:

BOY: Marcell Nagy
MR SÜTŐ: György Gazsó
FATHER: János Bán
STEPMOTHER: Judit Schell
ANNAMÁRIA: Sára Herrer
STEPMOTHER'S MOTHER: Olga Koós
TERKA: Piroska Molnár
UNCLE VILI'S WIFE: Ildikó Kishonti
UNCLE VILI: Miklós Benedek
UNCLE LAJOS: Péter Haumann
RELATIVE: László Baranyi
GRANDFATHER: Vilmos Kun
GRANDMOTHER: Márta Bakó
MALE RELATIVE: István Komlós
RELATIVE: Judit Meszléry
RELATIVE: Andrea Szoták
MR STEINER: Ádám Rajhona
MR FLEISCHMANN: György Barkó
MRS FLEISCHMANN: Kati Lázár
MOTHER: Ildikó Tóth

ANNAMÁRIA'S BROTHER:
Gáspár Mesés
POLICEMAN: József Szarvas
BOYS IN THE CUSTOMS HOUSE:
Jenő Nagy, Bence Bihari,
Patrik Holzmüller, Jakab Pilaszanovich,
Zoltán Tóth, Dániel Lugosi, Péter Bryja,
Krisztián Köles, Zsigmond Szilágyi,
Loránd Ács
ROZI: Zsolt Dér
SMOKER: Béla Dóra
PRETTY BOY: Bálint Péntek
MOSKOVICS: Dániel Szabó
LEATHER CRAFTSMAN:
Gergő Mészáros
HEDGE: Gábor Nyíri
FOREMAN: Ernő Fekete
EXPERT: István Gőz
UNLUCKY MAN: József Gyabronka
BITTER-FACED MAN:
Székely B. Miklós
SEAL FACE: Béla Spindler
GENDARME LIEUTENANT:
Krisztián Kolovratnik
MAN STANDING BY THE WINDOW:
György Hunyadkürti
CSARNAI: István Úri
STEAM: György Bősze
ZAKARIÁS: István Mészáros
STONE DRUNK GENDARME:
Géza Balkay
NEGOTIATING MAN: András Szegő
BODA: Géza Schramek
OLDER MAN: László Joó
GENDARME N.C.O.: László Jászai Jnr
GENDARME SERGEANTS: Zoltán
Dózsa, Áron Őze
TWO MEN WITH ARMBANDS:
Gábor Ferenczi, András Salamon
YOUNG GIRL'S MOTHER:
Ildikó Molnár
PACKING MAN: Antal Cserna
BOCSKOR: Zsolt Kovács
BARGAINING MAN: Péter Vallai
BALOGH: Zsolt László
GYULAI: Attila Magyar

LÉNÁRT: Péter Vida
ANOTHER MAN WITH ARMBAND:
András Surányi
RABBI: Sándor Halmágyi
PACKING WIFE: Éva Vándor
ERIKA: Adrien Táncos
BEREI: Zoltán Varga
WASP: Zoltán Bereczki
WOMAN STANDING BY THE
WINDOW: Kriszta Bíró
GEOGRAPHY TEACHER:
Ferenc Lengyel
SZABÓ: József Kelemen
YOUNG GIRL: Orsolya Tóth
FODOR: Tibor Mertz
CORRUPT GENDARME: Lajos Kovács
SELECTING SS OFFICER: Sándor Zsótér
PRISONER: Géza Tóth
MAN AT SELECTION: Géza Laczkovich
N.C.O.: Zoltán Barabás Kiss
CAPO: Attila Dolmány
BALDING MAN: Zoltán Bezerédi
OLD KOLLMANN: Endre Harkányi
OLDER KOLLMANN BOY:
Péter Fancsikai
YOUNGER KOLLMANN BOY:
Márton Brezina
CHOIR FROM KISVÁRDA: Mirkó
Andrassew, Viktor Csúcs, Máté Papp
PIANIST: Péter Göth
BANDI CITROM: Áron Dimény
PRISONER WITH ARMBAND:
Attila Besztercei
LAGER ÄLTESTER: Károly Nemcsák
FAZEKAS: Sándor Kőműves
THE FINN: András M. Kecskés
VI. BLOCKÄLTESTER: Lajos Kulcsár
SS SOLDIER: Szabolcs Thuróczy
SS N.C.O.: István Rimóczi
SÁNDOR: László Méhes
ROARING SS N.C.O.: József Lukács
SOLDIER TODT: Frank-Michael Köbe
BOSS: Péter Szokolay
HUNGARIAN DOCTOR: Pál Oberfrank
PFLEGER IN REHMSDORF:
Gergely Kocsis

PROTESTING MAN: Béla Paudits
TWO BATH ATTENDANTS:
László Kövesdi, Péter Richard
PJETYKA: Maciej Ciochki
HUNGARIAN PATIENT:
Ferenc Horváth
AMERICAN SERGEANT: Daniel Craig
UNCLE MIKLÓS: Gábor Máté
CAPTAIN: Dávid Szanitter
INTERPRETER: Csaba Gieler
REVEALED SS SOLDIER:
Máté Haumann
WOMAN AT RAILWAY STATION:
Anita Tóth
QUIZZING MAN: Miklós Molnár
BANDI CITROM'S SISTER:
Ági Olasz
BANDI CITROM'S MOTHER:
Mari Csomós
CONDUCTOR: József Jámbor
PROFESSIONAL MAN: Andor Lukács
UNKOWN WOMAN: Anikó Gruiz
Special thanks to Andrea Ladányi,
Tamás Dunai and Joe Bali (Berlin)

THE CREW

Production manager: Sándor Baló
Production co-ordinator: Edit Nagy
Assistant to director: Zoltán Bonta
Casting: Tamás Zilahy
Unit managers: Tamás Maros, Ákos Pesti,
Tamás Guba, László Rorárius
Office manager: Ágnes Kun
Production assistants: Attila Niklécy,
Mónika Bóta
Interpreter: Pálma Melis
Cashiers: Judit Kovács, Erzsébet Bodzsár
Assistants to Supervising Producer: Szonja
Domán, Péter Sarkadi
Second assistant director: Szabolcs Lang
Third assistant directors: Gergő Fülöp,
Zsófia Gonda
Cast arrangement: Eszter Fazekas
Diary: Gabi Antall
Art Directors: Zsuzsa Borvendég,
Judit Csák
Drawing artists: Beatrix Pethő,
Krisztina Szilágyi

Set dressing: Miklós Molnár
Second Set dressing: András Sinka,
Tamás Simon
Props: Ferenc Venczel, György Griger,
Gábor Postássy, János Cakó, Béla Tollay,
József Ócsai, László Sándor Sajerman
Construction managers: László Nagy,
József Kiss
Construction coordinators: László
Nagyidai, Miklós Schmelcz, Jnr.,
László Nagyidai, András Zsögön
1st set decorator: Pál Kozma
Construction duty: Csaba Vásári,
József Graczán, Antal Bobák
Scenic technician: Ferenc Ormos
Assistant scenic technician: Gábor Kiszelly
Technical duty: János Berki, Gábor Balog
Pyrotechnics: Gyula Krasnyánszky, Ferenc
Hábetler, Attila Érckövi, István Gittinger,
János Bujdosó, Gábor Csákovits,
Attila Varsányi
Make up artist: Kati Jakóts
Make up: Balázs Novák
Make up of extras: Noémi Czakó,
Réka Görgényi, Attiláné Járai,
Gábor Farkas, Nóra Koltai
Hair stylists: Erzsébet Rácz, Gaby
Németh, Jánosné Kajtár, Klára Szinek
Costume supervisor: Imre Orosz
Dressers: Gyula Zámbó, Péter Palotás,
Csaba Farkas, Attila Jánosi, Zsuzsa Tóth,
Mária Farkas, Ágnes Forgács,
János Géczi, Bea Makovits, Ferenc
Megyeri, Miklós Nemes, Mihály Sallai,
Gábor Szabó, Csaba Zollai
Boom operator: David Sutton
Sound assistants: Péter Schulteisz,
Szabolcs Stella
B camera: Zoltán Jánossa,
Balázs Bélafalvy
Focus Puller: Rawdon Hayne,
Brad Larner, Ádám Kliegl
1st assistant camera: Zoltán Jánossa,
Tamás Jánossa, David Mackie
Camera assistant: Sándor Domokos
Video operator: Ákos Gulyás

Gaffer: József Marton
Best Boy: József Simon, Károly Gaál
Sparks: Tibor Fazekas, István Faragó,
György Berghoffer, Ferenc Laczkó,
Attila Bartol, Zsigmond Molcsán,
Sándor Novák, Richard Szeidermann
Grip: Károly Brauner, Elek Hornyák,
István Bese
Photographer: Buda Gulyás
Further photographers: Wolfsberg Joseph,
Kerry Brown
Press relations: Zsolt Gréczy,
Charles MacDonald
Catering: Tamás Hungler
Production drivers: Csaba Lengyel, István
Meggyes, Barna Csonka, István Bodor,
Csaba Forgon, István Becságh,
István Varga, Pál Nyerges, Sándor Gera,
László Bálint, András Filó

Special thanks for the valuable
cooperation of Erika Tarr (production),
Rabbi Tamás Raj, László Gárdonyi
(railway expert), László Janicsek (assistant
director), Jenő Platschek, a resident of
Piliscsaba, and István Hajdú, former
deportee

SHOOTING IN GERMANY

Line Producer: Michael Reuter
Production managers: Anna von Wagner,
Michael Beier, Peter Hermann,
Tom Sternitzke
Casting Director: Heta Mantscheff
Art Director: Natalja Meier
Assistant Art Director: Lutz Hornig,
Christiane Stein
Props: Jan Rot, Sven Hausmann,
Marcus Berndt, Anja Simon
Set dressing: Claudia Kiefer,
Alex Munoz Gonzalez
Set construction: Ines Spain,
Axel Wieczorkowski
Construction duty: Lothar Heinert,

Ralf Jagnow, Maik Seemann,
Michael Reinemann, Thomas Specht,
Thomas Beier, Christl Geisemeyer,
Tom Hornig
Costume supervisors: Almut Stier,
Brigitte Rodriguez
Dressers: Petra Gärstke, Stefanie Pupke,
Jana Walther
Make up: Nadine Seidel, Ulrike Bomeier,
Cornelia Uhlemann, Heike Saal
Second Gaffer: Thomas Gosda
Second Best Boy: Hans Ulrich Graefe
Second Grip: Hardy Reichl
Sparks: André Schwemmin, Oliver Mehlis
Video operator: Ines Thomsen
Unit manager: Hildegard Westbeld
Production assistants:
Sören von der Heyde, Tommy Schlegel,
Timea Kiss Kovacs
Production drivers: Arved Maron, Marc
Eisenschink, Robert Hensel, Antje Seidel
Catering: Stephan Schneider, Ines Schultz,
Marco Schubert
Pyrotechnics: Roland Tropp
Script consultant: Amanda Mackenzie
Stuart
Military advisor: Péter Lippai

POST PRODUCTION

Post production Supervisor:
Jonathan Haren
Post production coordinator:
Edit Nagy
Assistant editor: Kati Juhász
Mixer: Martin Steyer
Sound Supervisor: Christian Conrad
Sound FX editor: Christian Conrad,
Jane Tattersall
Dialogue editor: Fabian Schmidt
Dubbing editor: Beate Hetenyi
Foley editor: Manuel Laval
Dubbing sound engineer (Hungary):
György Kovács
VFX consultant: Buda Gulyás

VFX Supervisor: Sven Martin
VFX Producer: Sacha Bertram
Studio Manager: Natascha Pfeiffer
Technical Director VFX: Jens Vielhaben
Music recording and mixing:
Fabio Venturi
Music recording organisation:
Enrico De Melis
Sound engineer/technical consultant:
Dénes Rédly
Pro Tools system engineer: Attila Kiss
Orchestra and choir: Orchestra and Choir
of the Hungarian Radio
Conductor: Kálmán Straussz
Manager: Gyula Krum
Soloist: Lisa Gerrard
Synthesiser: Ludovico Fulci
Pan-pipes: Ulrich Herkenhoff
Dulcimer: Ágnes Szakály
Recording and mixing made in
Studio 22 of Hungarian Radio
Music assistant to the director:
János Vészi
Digital colourist (Framestore CFC):
Adam Glasman

SPONSORS AND PRODUCERS

The film was sponsored by
Hungarian Motion Picture Public Fund,
Ministry of National Cultural Heritage,
Hungarian Historic Film Foundation,
MFG Filmförderung Baden-Württemberg,
Mitteldeutsche Medienförderung,
Ingenious Media plc,
Eurimages.
Cooproduction partners:
Hungarian Television Rt.,
Mitteldeutscher Rundfunk,
Hungarian Motion Picture Plc,
Magic Media Rt.,
EuroArts Medien GmbH.,
Renegade Films, Inc.

Year of production: 2003–2004.

CONVERSATION IN BERLIN WITH IMRE KERTÉSZ ABOUT FATELESS AND THE CINEMA

ACQUAINTANCE

We talked in the cafe of the Kempinski Hotel in Berlin from 6 p.m. on Friday
23 July 2004. Imre Kertész arrived with Madam Magda precisely on time.
He had no objection to the use of a tape recorder, moreover, he agreed that
the small group receiving him could also take part in the conversation.
   We first talked about his initial meeting with Lajos Koltai.

I can tell you how we first met. However, we must go back a bit in time, back to
when someone thought of making a film of *Fateless*. It was a long time ago.
Most probably, a man from an American television company made an inquiry
with Magdi. Then Péter Gothár was keen to film it, but we never got as far as the
screenplay. In the end the dream, to put it like that because nothing was real at the
time, started to become more concrete when a company in Munich became
involved. What happened was that Magic Media and the company in Munich
together went ahead with *Fateless*. If I remember well, the Munich company had
eighty per cent and Magic Media had twenty. I was asked if I wanted to take part
in writing the screenplay. I did not, because I thought of the film as something
I could not have anything to do with in practice. It is impossible to adapt the novel
because the language, which actually represents the novel, cannot be put on the
screen. Thus I decided that I would not have anything to do with the film. If they
want to do it, alright, I would grant them the rights but they should not expect
anything else from me. So they chose a British scriptwriter whom I met, together
with the representatives of Magic Media and the Munich company in one of the
Sípos restaurants, or somewhere in Old Buda. We had a curd cheese pasta and
drank a glass of wine. We were making friends with the Brit who seemed to have
understood everything and was soon ready with the script. It was deadly. It begins
with a world famous violinist with a huge black hat sitting in a taxi and crossing
Margaret Bridge. He looks down at the Danube and starts remembering things
which are not in the book at all.

   The chap did not understand from the start that the technique of the novel was
linear. So if the story does not develop linearly but he interrupts it and leaves
something out then the essence is simply lost. Thus I protested against the script
and I had to do my best to stop the thing, because, of course, the British chap had
a contract which gave him the right to all sorts of compensation. He had to be
paid, but at least we got rid of that horrible script.

   Then János Szász cropped up as an idea. Magic Media brought him and we got
acquainted. I knew his father well, Péter was a good friend of mine, especially
when he worked for the radio. I and my friends worked a lot for Péter, so I was a
bit moved that his son was going to be involved with *Fateless*. What had happened
before showed me clearly that if a foreigner was commissioned to write the script it
could only be spoilt. Obviously, no professional scriptwriter will settle for
following the story in a linear way. They all want to include a trick, some special
about-turn twist. For example, from back to front, from front to middle and so on.
That would not do. So I asked my friend György Spiró for his dramaturgical

advice. Let him tell me what could be done with *Fateless*. We sat down and using his advice we created something that could well be regarded as a base. Meanwhile the Munich company went bankrupt and dropped the film. I don't know how come, since I don't understand business matters, moreover I don't even want to know them – and I don't take part in those matters. Magic Media had bought the rights. However, at a certain moment I lost my trust in János Szász. I had to realise that Szász's relationship to the novel was not right. He could not step back, keep his distance, whereas my intention regarding the novel involved precisely that distance – the absolutely calm and dispassionate objectivity, which irritates many, but that is the essence of the novel. Of course, the distance cannot be achieved with 'resentment'.

   That's where we were when Zsuzsa Radnóti rang me up and asked whether I felt like going over for dinner because Lajos Koltai, the noted director of photography was going to be there. So we appeared at her place and *Fateless* was brought up. I told Lajos, who I liked very much at first sight, that at the moment we were in a crisis and what if he would take *Fateless* in hand. So to say the idea was raised by all, by Zsuzsa Radnóti, by Magdi, all of us suggested it. That's how this very warm friendship began and has been lasting since.

Madam Magda, a dear guest on the first day of shooting

THE LETTER

I mentioned in passing that I knew of a letter which was written by Imre Kertész. I knew its content but unfortunately it had not turned up so far. Lajos Koltai remembers that Imre Kertész wrote a type of letter which can only be written by a writer. It addresses everyone at the same time and everyone had a sentence addressed to him alone. It is important because János Szász, in an interview dated 12 March 2004, said that he had met the owner of Magic Media half a year after Imre Kertész's decision. The owner was a bit embarrassed, then he declared: "the situation is that Kertész doesn't want you to make the film…" Szász replied: "That's OK, but you and Kertész should have told me. He who fires someone should deem it right to tell the fired person, even if he does receive the Nobel Prize later." If it happened in this way, it means that the producer 'swallowed' the letter.

I really did write a letter to Magic Media; the letter should be looked for, there. I stated clearly that I had a crisis of confidence regarding János Szász and I would like Lajos Koltai to direct the film, and so on, in detail. The letter was also motivated by the fact that Lajos clearly said – and I regard this as very important to state now – that as long as we did not clarify the matter with Szász or we did not clarify the Szász-matter he would not join. I can truly say that Lajos highly appreciated Szász, not in the past tense but in the present. In the event, the matter was sorted out quickly. Magic Media acknowledged the content of the letter and Lajos and János met and talked to each other. From that moment on we were able to believe that we were going to make a film of *Fateless*.

The fate of the letter had intrigued me throughout and Imre Kertész, although he did not believe he could find it, promised he would try. Therefore the fax he sent on 28 August 2004 pleased me unexpectedly. "This is to let you know that I have found my letter of 29 June 2000, written to Péter Barbalics, in which I asked him to commission Lajos Koltai to direct the film Fateless *instead of János Szász. The attached text is the copy of the original fax so it is 100 per cent authentic." With the author's permission, the letter written to Péter Barbalics is as follows:*

"Dear Péter, with reference to our telephone conversation, I hereby confirm in writing: to my greatest regret, I have lost my confidence in János Szász as the potential director of the film of *Fateless*.

"My simple reason for this is that for three years since the adaptation of my novel to a film was first mentioned Jani Szász has not added anything apart from the initial enthusiasm. György Spiró wrote the script alone or together with me. Szász did not seem to be interested what we were to come up with. The few ideas or limited concept I heard from him, in your company, convinced me that he was not approaching the material in the spirit of the novel. He did not even try to really imagine how the philosophy of the novel and its language can be transposed into a film. I believe he is too busy to have time for it. I know how committed to the stage he is and I have heard of the welcome news that he is going to direct in America, visit workshops, etc. And that he is making a documentary for Spielberg, in connection with which I would remark briefly that there is no bigger contradiction than the one between Spielberg's approach and that of *Fateless*.

"Nevertheless time flies and you are going to set the date for filming soon. Well, making a film of *Fateless* is a task which requires deep knowledge and preparation. There is a type of education which belongs to the Holocaust as culture (this is the title of one of my essays) and I have come to the conclusion that Jani Szász does not have the education as much as he does not have his own concept on this world trauma. In this way it is impossible to set out on a job which is based on a strict budget and does not tolerate a creative method of daily improvisations. I have no doubt that we are facing that unless we change the director now.

"Lajos Koltai happened to phone me recently. He has read the novel and briefly he rather likes it; he is thinking about it and his talking about it has convinced me that he has understood the depth and has created a vision for film, which exactly tallies with mine. He also liked the script. However, in no way does he want to obstruct János Szász's path. I had to tell him that before I had talked to him, actually before I had met him at all, I had already let you know that I did not want to work together with János Szász. I ensured him that it was not his arrival which convinced me about having to change directors but the above mentioned facts. Thus Koltai cannot be accused of taking any part in our relieving János Szász from directing *Fateless*. Both Koltai and I respect Szász, not to mention his having been Koltai's pupil. I agreed that I would clarify the matter with you. I have done it in this letter and declare in the present situation I do not want or intend to work with Jani Szász – it is not at all because I do not like him or doubt his talent, but purely because he is not prepared for the job.

"Then again, once the situation is like this I definitely ask you to include Lajos Koltai in the work promptly and commission him to direct the film. I am convinced that Koltai's concept is uniquely authentic, he does not display any sense of resentment or accusation but is led by one thing only, which also guided me when I wrote the novel, and that is the depiction of a pure soul as it is trying to find sense amidst senselessness.

"I hope I have managed to convince you that we cannot hesitate for long in our own best interest – serious work must be started with someone who is willing, and that person is Lajos Koltai."

DREAMS

Lajos first looked through the script written by Spiró and me very quickly, practically in two weeks. He read it and we discussed it in detail. But I immediately told him it was incomplete and as soon as the situation happens to turn serious there will be a script that would make the film possible.

That was when something started which we can call the struggle for finance.

In reality we were still day-dreaming. We got together from time to time in order to keep in touch. Three of us sat down in the Rózsakert café on the Hill of Roses, had some coffee, and were weaving far-reaching plans, but nothing was really happening. There was no money. However, the many discussions made it clear, and I have included it in the script, that we were not going to make a Holocaust film. The Holocaust cannot be made on film. We want to film the depersonalised fateless. The story is the way of a soul. This road a person, a child, goes on is the way of depersonalisation. He loses his personality and his way leads through the concentration camp. As far as this aspect is concerned, it's naturally a Holocaust film but in no way does it want to claim to 'resolve' the Holocaust as the Holocaust issue – in the case that *Fateless* on film becomes heated through and opens up, so to say, it becomes comprehensive, that is general, interpretable generally such that we interpret the whole period, the dictatorship, and so on. But we do not intend to depict the Holocaust, since we do not have any experience of the inside of a gas chamber, and the Holocaust can be described only by those who went through it. Thus we made a very important distinction right at the start, I think it was the decisive step so that the film could be started at all. ... Meanwhile Lajos pronounced a significant sentence. In so far as it can happen to anyone that they are taken off a bus and thus their life is changed in a decisive way, the film is absolutely relevant. It can happen today, during the age of terrorism.

From a writer's point of view what Spiró and I created was important since we reviewed the material dramaturgically, that is whether the novel can at all be adapted to a script. We did not go into detail at the time because the film was not approaching reality. The situation was different with Lajos. He definitely made me feel like writing the script. I felt so close to Lajos, we understood each other exactly, both of us saw what we were talking about and I knew that Lajos was going to make the film which was also my ideal, which was neither extreme, touching on the avant-garde, nor Hollywood trash. Lajos and I already discussed it at the very beginning. We used phrases like 'emotional but not sentimental'. We regarded stealthy sentimentalism as the first danger to overcome; it's a danger which usually characterises child descriptions. I felt that Lajos could adapt the novel to film, the question only was whether anything could be taken over from the novel. That was my problem and I had to resign myself to the fact, or I myself determine what I wanted to include from the novel. I cannot take on the impossible. So I had to indicate exactly what I want to see on film, which is essentially the story of the loss of personality.

THE SCRIPT IS READY

I gave my opinion about the problems connected with a script and concretely with my case in the preface of the German edition. It's a pity this is not printed in the Hungarian edition. It would be more precisely understandable what the difference is between the script and the novel. In short, the writer creates a universe from sentences and words in the novel. It is a world he creates. But the writer hands over a blank cheque to the director in the case of a script, because the director will create a world with words, faces, actors, music and so on. I know not everyone thinks like that, but this viewpoint is a result of my own experience. If I had wanted to write the same in the script as in the novel I would not have written anything. The novel is a completely ready, closed form which cannot be divided and cannot be filmed. In order to do that language would have to be filmed or at least such methods of transposing the material would have to be found which may not be about what I would like to say. So I had to define exactly what could be put in the script, resulting in it still being similar to the novel.

No doubt I was able to write the script at all because there was the rapport between Lajos and me. Although I am not a professional scriptwriter, I made every effort for the script to inspire him so that he could make the film from it; more precisely, so that he would be able to translate it into the reality of pictures. If I had forced him to film the novel we would not have got anywhere.

A special condition tempted me into the scriptwriter's role, which was partly alien and which partly traumatised me since you return to a finished novel, which had stood several tests and which I wrote thirty years ago, with great difficulty. That special condition was Lajos himself, who was enthusiastic all along. Actually I could say silently enthusiastic, because he did not say anything special, like "let's do it" or "it's going to be a box office hit". But both of us knew what we were doing, both of us knew what we each had taken on. This rapport was needed for me to start writing the script. As we know, the end result was not an unambiguous success. First of all Hungarian reviewers scorned the script and if they wrote about it they said I had betrayed the novel and so on – in other words, nonsense. Of course, after I had received the Nobel Prize I could not stand before those so-called critics who

want to see me account for myself. It is not worth dealing with that.
On the contrary, let me call your attention to an article by a noted film reviewer,
Fritz Göttler, published in the *Süddeutsche Zeitung* in spring 2003.
He understands what it is about, he sees exactly what the golden light,
the silent irreality represents at the end of the script, which we had to see
in the camp once and which will
awake future memory.

Those literary people who read
a script like a piece of literature, a
novel, don't understand at all that
they could express their opinion
only when they see what the
director has done. I do not think
a script can be judged until the film
is ready.

The writer plays a very different
role – I hope I'm not boring you
with the repetition – when writing
a script or a novel. What is not
linguistically radical enough in the
film's script is radical in the novel
and can be radical in pictures at the
same time.

With his wife on
the terrace of the
Sándor Palace in
the Buda Castle

THE FILM IS ROLLING

*This thought leads us to the story of making the film. We make a big leap.
The script was published in 2001 and Imre Kertész did not take part in the
procedures concerning the film apart from offering his supporting sympathy.
He was busy enough with writing his novel* Settlement. *Of course, he was paying
attention to what was happening with the film, moreover on every possible
occasion when he was interviewed he gave his support to Lajos Koltai's
undertaking. However, he did not have any direct influence on the fact that the
first shooting day was set for 15 December 2003.*

When we began, that is when Lajos started shooting the film, we agreed
that he had a free hand with the monologues and also the dialogues.
This was very important because the script contained too much. Many
scenes contain a lot of dialogues but when the actor appears his face reveals
much and certain things become unnecessary. So I told Lajos not to keep to
the script, leave the text out where required as the pictures dictate. Yes, the
pictures, because I immediately saw how expressive his images were. There is
absolutely no need to speak over expressive pictures. So he encouraged me to be

flexible when writing the script and I did the same in return with the shooting. I think I was right, since I accept that the script disappears page by page while filming takes place. A film is not a literary genre. A film belongs to the director. No doubt about that.

So we must accept that certain episodes of the linearly built story represent stations from the director's aspect, according to Lajos Koltai. They override the story of a way of the cross. 'How is religious symbolism included here?', we may ask, but let us rather accept that this approach is not alien to the writer, either.

I accept it because if you read the texts I wrote for my own novel, and similar texts can be found in my book *Someone Else*, then I also approach the matter religiously. But this does not mean anything in terms of the film, it is only philosophically like this. The pictures will decide what is done in this respect. I have seen the rushes and it seemed to me to have been done. Because it was as if I had seen two things simultaneously. On the one hand, there is the story which is happening and, on the other, it is as if a requiem was taking place. It is the magic of the pictures and that certain distance which can be so fertile to allow such pictures to be made, to have such experience. I hope that this experience remains after seeing the finished film. How events are happening and how nature surrounds them is very moving. The feeling of bereavement makes the requiem real for our inner hearing. Naturally I had been expecting these pictures but could not imagine them. I am not good at films. I enjoy them but do not make them. The point for me was that Lajos Koltai deeply understands the concept, understands the way of the cross and sees why the golden dust cloud flies around the deportees who are returning to the camp from work, and I knew that Lajos was able to show and use it in the film.

He told me his ideas about the picture, They were beautiful, for example, that the film was going to be in colour at the beginning, then getting grey and at the end it was going to regain increasingly full colours. Thus, so to say, I knew the pictorial script but I could not imagine it. Of course, I suggested that the pictures should be authentic and all the clothes, every object and building, etc. would bear the image of authenticity. We both considered that important since we have had bad experiences. We have seen films with the disappointing scene where a quite fat person wearing a striped costume is standing by a thin wire fence and calls to someone: "Hello, Mr Schindler!". And they have the cheek to write that it is Auschwitz. We wanted something absolutely authentic in this respect. And Lajos has done extremely well. He did not use any special effects but built up the camp. Moreover, he built it so authentically that when I entered the hospital barrack, which I think was constructed in Fót, I was filled with terror, it was so similar to the original.

The appropriate pictures will be appealing in the film. Is it possible to have pleasing pictures in relation to this theme?

That is the spirit of the novel. Nature has a role in the story all along. The film, just like nature, has this beauty in that the pictures are not made beautiful but are really so; including suffering. So we are not talking about innocent beauty. It is an extraordinary idea to have the collapse on Appellplatz depicted by a dancer. It is real and unreal at the same time ... and at the same time horrible. We should not think that if the story takes place in a concentration camp we must give up art and that only stinking reality exists.

It is unnecessary to express ourselves by going into monstrosities, because that is not how the book expresses itself. There are hardly any 'horrible details' in the book. This is not what is horrible. The language is that.

The boy feeling homesick is terrible. His happiness is horrible. These elements must be found and not pictures like a guard punching someone yet again or a deportee being kicked once more. The dancer's fantastic movement, a snail movement pointing to the end, the body's twisting expresses the essential horror in pictures to me.

Imre Kertész at the shooting on 17 December 2003

Lajos Koltai had laid great emphasis on irony in an earlier concept.

That was not executed. How to say, that would be another film. Irony is carried by language in the novel. It's in concepts like honesty. It cannot be done in a film. If we had put emphasis on that, half the script would have contained what joke belonged to which notion. For example, it is an ironic concept when they are sitting at the table in the beginning of the novel and looking at his father the boy is disgusted by him. In vain do I do it literally, something else will show in the film. It is not ironic. What does not astonish the reader in the text astonishes him in the pictures. Irony makes everything obvious, everything can be only ironic.

That is what I was afraid of with Gothár, for example, whom, by the way, I liked very much, but I could have been apprehensive that he would emphasise only the grotesque, which is, however, only one aspect of the novel, because grotesque, drama, the impossible situation, being exposed and time are all present simultaneously in the novel.

When shooting the director used the depiction of cruelty rather economically. For example, the slap the boy receives is important in the novel. Koltai thought that if he had depicted plenty of horror before, the slap would not be worth anything. Slow increase is the point. Man is first deprived of his freedom, then he starves, becomes full of lice, wounds are inflicted and so on.

The metamorphosis the child goes through is quite shocking in the film. In the first pictures we see an angel-like boy who turns into a bald and scarred child, and this change also expresses the inner story, the way of the soul.

The script already made it clear that Gyuri Köves's way home became emphatic. Lajos Koltai underlined its importance several times during shooting. The way back in the novel, however, is expressed not so much in scenes but by language.

Yes, indeed. Returning home is like the reverse of a piece of music. It is made of the same notes but sounds differently. It sounds backwards. The locations and characters at the end are varieties of the same material which appear in the first chapter. But there are characters in the novel who do not play an important role in the film. However, it is extremely important to show the drama of the way back in the film. This question faced us all along. There is a scene on the tram with the well-known answer in the novel to a journalist's question concerning what Gyuri Köves feels again at home, seeing the city. This scene was absent in the script. We included it afterwards. I increased the significance of the way back home in the script. This was demanded by the objectivity of the film. We must not forget what Europe and the way home really looked like after the war. When the former deportees flooded the roads and one after the other they discovered in their own lines SS members who mixed in with those who were going home. Then there was the country itself, Germany and 'resentment', which we see completely differently today sixty years after the war. Today we already know what an 'outstanding' Rákosi cadre, resentment will make of the character of Uncle Miklós.

Why was Imre Kertész so rarely present at the shooting?

I am sure I would have disturbed things. The author always disturbs. When I was first there we clarified a lot concerning what to leave out. Besides that, I did not have anything to do at the shooting. If I cannot contribute with any positive activity to a shooting day, then why on earth be under their feet? Everyone is looking for a chair for me; I leave my glasses by the camera then everyone is looking for them; there is no point to my presence. People were enthusiastic without me. Lajos, for example, was full of energy and vitality, he explained even to the last extra what the scene was about and what had to be done. In any case, I was not involved in the casting either, partly because it is not me who is working with them and partly since I do not even know them. I had only one protégé, Joe Bali, who is a pastry-cook here in Berlin and whenever I passed his shop he always came out to ask me about having a role in the film. I couldn't resist that nice young man. Otherwise, I didn't interfere in the casting. When filming had to stop I was very sorry for Lajos, who was really broken, meaning his nerves and soul, too. Nevertheless, he considerately left me out of that business.

IMRE KERTÉSZ, THE VIEWER

During the conversation it struck me that Imre Kertész referred to himself as a viewer. As the 'gentleman writes', the 'viewer watches'. But what? Dozens of interviews were done with Kertész concerning Fateless, *but no one thought of asking: "Dear Mr writer, what about the cinema? What is your relationship to the cinema?"*

Really, I was not asked. Are you asking me? What relationship can one have to the cinema? I was a child when the first colour film was shown. It was on in the Elite cinema, on the Buda side of Margaret Bridge where there is a shabby cinema called the Bem today. It used to be a very good cinema for the residents of Buda, an elegant audience. I saw the first film in colour there, some kind of Western. I don't remember the title but I do remember some famous star, John Wayne or someone from an earlier generation, was walking on top of a train with a Colt in his hand to rob, I think, the passengers.

Introducing Miklós Molnár, who furnished the Köves flat in the studio in the spirit of the novel

Film was magic for me. I also saw Leni Riefenstahl's Olympic film. I was absolutely amazed by it as a child and I did not perceive it as political propaganda. One of the biggest shocks in my childhood, at the age of ten, was when we booked tickets for *The Thief of Baghdad,* but meanwhile Hungary had joined the war and *Baron Münchhausen* was on instead. I saw the former only after 1945 when I returned from the camp.

I love the cinema very much. As an author I was never imagining I was writing a script, being part of film-making, but my way of thinking, just like that of every person living in the 20th century, is obviously influenced by cinematographic images and the atmosphere of films, namely everything that you receive from a film, the real dream world, so to say, without which life cannot be imagined today. We all perform a little in films; it's a bit like thinking ourselves to be the private detective in pulp fiction. Films decisively contribute to how we feel and the way we move around in the world.

A great film experience in my adulthood happened in 1957, in the summer following the revolution. I was having a holiday at a dusty place near Siófok by Lake Balaton, and I was thinking of how I could spend the evening at the end of an empty, very hot day. An Italian film was on at the open-air cinema. "An Italian film can only be good," I said and bought a ticket. I sat in the cinema a little tired and a little bored. A film began and I was dumbstruck already with the very first frames. It was *The Road*. I thought that if it was an Italian film it would be a comedy. What I saw lacked any introduction because nobody talked about the greatness of the film, the film had not been advertised and at the time no one knew the names of either the actors or the director, Fellini. What I saw was so astonishing that I saw it again once or twice. To me it was an experience in film like Camus in literature, whose work was not known in Hungary by anyone until his novel *The Outsider* was published in Budapest in 1957.

Then I saw a series from the films of the French New Wave in the 1960s. They were on in the former Broadway cinema, called Filmmuzeum then. Let me mention about the cinema that it was advertised during the war as a bomb-proof film theatre. And it was the first cinema in Hungary with air conditioning. Anyway, the French films were on there. And so that people could not see them the performances began at 9 a.m. I remember we got up at six every morning and I saw the most significant films of the French New Wave. *The 400 Blows* and *The Cousins*. And *Hiroshima, mon amour*. It was fantastic, with a fantastic actress.

So films played an important role in my life. Despite the fact that I am a language-centred person, I can fit it in to thinking in pictures. Thus I enjoyed films by Resnais, which are precise, boring yet very thrilling. What I admire in films is that the cinema is an extremely flexible and attractive genre. Not speaking about Bergman's and Fellini's films. Antonioni's *The Night*, for example, is a basic piece which provided me almost with a literary experience. Its structure also reflects an astonishing dramaturgical approach.

When I came home in 1945 one went to the cinema instead of school. And we couldn't get enough of war films. I also liked detectives, then came *The Stranger* ... *Citizen Kane* was a later experience.

In my childhood I liked silly entertaining films from among the Hungarian films. What was the title of one? *The Lady's a Little Crazy* ... It was made in 12 days. They were sweet. Then when Arrow-Cross-like films began to appear I didn't like them. The appealing actor Antal Páger was in the film *István Bors*. That was hard. But a Jewish family would go and see this film, too. Moreover, when the yellow star had to be worn there were certain cinemas where anyone with a yellow star was banned from entering. Think about the complete absurdity of the matter – you were wearing a yellow star and thus you couldn't go to the Atrium cinema, say, but you could go to the small dirty one on Rákóczi Road, and Jews went and saw *István Bors* and the even more Arrow Cross films with Zita Szeleczky.

And then how much Antal Páger was celebrated in the 1960s when he returned to Hungary.

But let's stay with films. András Jeles directed an excellent film, *The Tragedy of Man*. It was a great experience for me. I was enthusiastic about it. The film *Love* by Károly Makk was a rather nice film. Then there were Miklós Jancsó's films. I saw nearly all. *The Confrontation* and *Agnus dei* are unforgettable. I don't share the notion that nothing can be depicted in a dictatorship. If it is good, it is good. No doubt about that. If they show it today they are also good. And *Agnus dei* and *The Confrontation* are both good films. The latter spoke to me as if personally, since I knew that group of people in white shirts. I saw *The Carousel* in its time and it was also an appealing film. I like Szabó's *Father* and I also liked *Taking Sides*. So, my 'relationship' to films, so to say, has always been normal in respect of my age and the circumstances.

Recorded by *József Marx*

FILMOGRAPHY

YEARS OF LEARNING (1965–1969)

- **THE FENCE,** amateur film (1965)
- **IMPROVISATION,** amateur film (1965)
- **STEEL WORKERS,** examination film (1966)
  Directed by Tamás Farkas, camera: Lajos Koltai
  College of Drama and Film, black and white, 16 mm, 13 min.
- **THE HOLIDAY,** examination day (1966)
  Directed by Lajos Koltai, camera: Gyula Gazdag
  College of Drama and Film, black and white, 6 min.
- **ON THE SEVENTH DAY,** examination film (1966)
  Directed and camera by Lajos Koltai
  College of Drama and Film, black and white, 16 mm. 13 min.
- **HIPPODROME,** examination film (1966)
  Directed by Tamás Farkas, camera: Lajos Koltai
  College of Drama and Film, black and white, 13 min
- **PRELUDE,** examination film (1966)
  Directed by Gyula Gazdag, camera; Lajos Koltai
  College of Drama and Film, black and white, 19 min.
- **SILENT NIGHT,** examination film (1967)
  Directed by Tamás Farkas, camera: Lajos Koltai
  Cast: Ildikó Pécsi, András Kern, Nándor Tomanek
  College of Drama and Film, black and white, 22 min.
- **BORDERS,** examination film (1968)
  Directed and written by Maja Borisova, camera: Lajos Koltai
  College of Drama and Film, black and white, 17 min.
- **THREE GIRLS,** examination film (1968)
  Directed by Dezső Magyar, camera: Lajos Koltai
  College of Drama and Film, black and white, 16 mm, 40 min.
- **EXPRESS ADVENTURE,** advertising film (1969)
  Directed by Tamás Farkas, camera: Lajos Koltai
  College of Drama and Film, colour, 27 min.

AT THE BORDERS OF DOCUMENTARIES AND FEATURES (1969–1974)

- **AGITATORS,** feature (1969)
  Directed by Dezső Magyar, camera: Lajos Koltai
  Cast: Gábor Bódy, László Földes, László Bertalan, Tamás Szentjóby, Péter Dobai, György Cserhalmi, Sándor Oszter, András Kozák, Márk Zala, György Pintér, Gábor Révai
  Balázs Béla Studio, black and white, 78 min.
- **INDECENT PHOTO-GRAPHS,** documentary (1970)
  Directed by Géza Böszörményi, camera: Lajos Koltai, István Zöldi
  Mafilm Report and Documentary Studio, black and white, 17 min.
- **GIRLS,** documentary (1970)
  Directed by György Szomjas, camera: Lajos Koltai, Mihály Halász
  Mafilm Report and Documentary Studio, black and white, 18 min.
- **HONEYMOONS,** report film (1970)
  Directed by György Szomjas, camera: Lajos Koltai, Mihály Halász
  Balázs Béla Studio, black and white, 38 min.
- **THE PRESS,** feature (1971)
  Directed by Gyula Maár, camera: Lajos Koltai
  Cast: István Szilárdy, Mari Törőcsik, Tibor Szilágyi, Mária Gór Nagy
  Balázs Béla Studio, black and white, 16 mm, 71 min.
- **THE ARCHAIC TORSO,** experimental documentary (1971)
  Directed by Péter Dobai, camera: Lajos Koltai
  Balázs Béla Studio, black and white, 35 min.
- **THE THIRD,** experimental documentary (1971)
  Directed by Gábor Bódy, camera: Lajos Koltai
  Balázs Béla Studio, black and white, 48 min.
- **IN THE LŐRINC SPINNING-MILL,** documentary (1971)
  Directed by Márta Mészáros, camera: Lajos Koltai
  Mafilm Report and Documentary Studio, black and white, 18 min.
  Prizes: Leipzig, Documentary

Festival: recognition by
the jury,
Miskolc, Festival of Short
Films and Documentaries:
Main Prize of the trade union
• **TO WHOM IT MAY
CONCERN,** documentary
(1971)
Directed by Lívia Gyarmathy,
written by Géza Böszörményi,
camera: Lajos Koltai
Mafilm Report and
Documentary Studio,
black and white, 16 min.
Prizes: Krakow: Silver Dragon
main prize,
Miskolc: prize of the
Documentary and Report Film
Category
• **ANNA BALL IN FÜRED,**
documentary (1972)
Directed by György Szomjas,
camera: Lajos Koltai
Mafilm Report and
Documentary Studio, HTV,
black and white, 15 min.
Prizes: Miskolc: prize of the
Documentary and Report Film
Category
• **HUNGARIAN HOLIDAY,**
commercial (1972)
Directed by György Szomjas,
camera: Lajos Koltai
Mafilm Publicity Film Studio,
colour, 16 min.
• **SÁROSPATAK,** documentary
(1972)
Directed by Ferenc Kardos,
camera: Lajos Koltai
Mafilm Documentary Studio,
black and white, 20 min.
HIGH ALTITUDE,
documentary (1972)
Directed by Ferenc Téglásy,
camera: Lajos Koltai
Balázs Béla Studio,
black and white, 18 min.
• **SOMETHING ELSE,**
documentary (1972)
Directed by Pál Erdőss,
camera: Lajos Koltai

Balázs Béla Studio,
black and white, 30 min.
• **WAIT A SEC!,** feature (1973)
Directed by Lívia Gyarmathy,
written by Lívia Gyarmathy
and Géza Böszörményi,
camera: Lajos Koltai
Cast: Miklós Markovich,
Elma Bulla, Sándor Horváth,
Eva Ras, József Madaras,
Ádám Szirtes, Tibor Szilágyi,
László Dózsa, József Mentes,
Ildikó Bánsági
Budapest Feature Film Studio,
colour
Prizes: Prize of Hungarian
Film Critics for best
supporting actress to Eva Ras;
Panama: special prize
• **EXCERCISES,** documentary
(1973)
Directed by György Szomjas,
written by István Kardos,
camera: Lajos Koltai
Balázs Béla Studio,
black and white, 25 min.
• **RIDDANCE,** feature
(1973)
Directed by Márta Mészáros,
camera: Lajos Koltai
Cast: Erzsébet Kútvölgyi,
Gábor Nagy, Ferenc Kállai,
Mari Szemes, Kati Lázár
Hunnia Feature Film Studio,
black and white
• **AT THE END OF THE
ROAD,** feature (1973)
Directed by Gyula Maár,
written by András Bíró,
camera: Lajos Koltai
Cast: Jozef Króner,
László Szacsvay, Mari
Törőcsik, Lajos Őze,
Tamás Major, Lili Monori,
Dezső Garas, Tibor Szilágyi
Hunnia Feature Film Studio,
black and white
Prizes: Toulon: FICC Jury
Prize, Prize for Best Direction;
Budapest: Hungarian Film
Critics' Prize for best actor to

Jozef Króner, for best first
feature to Gyula Maár
• **THE CAR,** feature (1974)
Directed by Géza
Böszörményi, camera:
Lajos Koltai
Cast: Eva Ras, Jácint Juhász,
Hédi Temessy, Dezső Garas,
Károly Kovács
Hunnia Feature Film Studio,
colour
• **ON THE RUN,** feature
(1974)
Directed by Lajos Fazekas,
written by Ákos Kertész,
camera: Lajos Koltai
Cast: Katalin Gyöngyössy,
Péter Huszty, Iván Darvas,
Ildikó Pécsi, Irma Patkós
Hunnia Feature Film Studio,
colour
• **RECRUITS,** documentary
(1974)
Directed by Pál Erdőss,
camera: Lajos Koltai
Balázs Béla Studio,
black and white, 38 min.
• **HOLIDAY IN BRITAIN,**
documentary feature (1974)
Directed by István Dárday,
camera: Lajos Koltai
Budapest Feature Film Studio,
colour
Prizes: Budapest: Hungarian
Film Critics' prize for Best
Direction, for Best Camera to
Lajos Koltai; Mannheim:
Grand Prix

**THE MASTER OF
ATMOSPHERE (1975–1980)**

• **THE NATURAL HISTORY
OF AN INDIVIDUAL CASE,**
documentary (1975)
Directed by Szalai Györgyi,
camera: Lajos Koltai
Balázs Béla Studio,
black and white, 107 min.

- **MRS DÉRY, WHERE ARE YOU?**, feature (1975)
Directed by Gyula Maár, written by János Pilinszky, camera: Lajos Koltai
Cast: Mari Törőcsik, Ferenc Kállai, Mária Sulyok, Imre Ráday, Tamás Major
Prizes: Budapest: Hungarian Film Critics Prize for Best Cameraman to Lajos Koltai, Best Actress to Mari Törőcsik; Cannes: Prize for Best Actress to Mari Törőcsik

- **EPIDEMIC**, feature (1975)
Directed by Pál Gábor, camera: Lajos Koltai
Cast: András Kozák, Ion Bog, László Szacsvay, Gábor Reviczky
Budapest Feature Film Studio, colour
Prizes: Cairo: Grand Prix

- **ADOPTION**, feature (1975)
Directed by Márta Mészáros, written by Ferenc Grunwalsky, Gyula Hernádi, camera: Lajos Koltai
Cast: Kati Berek, Gyöngyvér Vigh, Péter Fried
Hunnia Feature Film Studio, colour
Prizes: Berlin: 'Golden Bear', Otto Dibelius Prize; Chicago: Gold Plaque

- **DER LETZTE TANZLEHRER (The Last Teacher of Dance)**, TV film (1975)
Directed by Géza Böszörményi, camera: Lajos Koltai
Cast: Ági Bánfalvi, Ferenc Bencze
Zweites Deutsches Fernsehen-Mafilm, International Studio, colour

- **ON THE SIDE-LINE**, feature (1976)
Directed by Péter Szász, camera: Lajos Koltai

Cast: Ferenc Kállai, Gyula Bodrogi, Tamás Andor, Péter Haumann, Judit Meszléry
Hunnia Feature Film Studio, colour
Prizes: Tehran: Prize for Best Actor to Ferenc Kállai

- **FLARE AND FLICKER**, feature (1976)
Directed by Gyula Maár, camera: Lajos Koltai
Cast: Mari Törőcsik, Ági Mészáros, Lenke Lorán, Stefan Kvietik, József Bihari, Jozef Króner
Hunnia Feature Film Studio, colour
Prizes: Taormina: Prize for Best Actress to Mari Törőcsik

- **THE WOMAN OF LŐCSE IN WHITE**, TV film adaptation of the novel by Mór Jókai (1976)
Directed by Gyula Maár, camera: Lajos Koltai
Cast: Mari Törőcsik, József Madaras, Tibor Szilágyi, Stefan Kvietik, Kornél Gelley, Hédi Temessy, Tamás Dunai
Mafilm-HTV, colour

- **THE AMERICAN CIGARETTE**, feature (1977)
Directed by János Dömölky, written by István Csurka, camera: Lajos Koltai
Cast: Hilda Gobbi, Zoltán Makláry
Budapest Studio-HTV, colour

- **FILM NOVEL**, documentary-feature (1977)
Directed by István Dárday, camera: Lajos Koltai, Ferenc Pap
Mafilm Budapest Studio, black and white
Prizes: Budapest: Hungarian Film Critics' Prize for Best Film, Prize for Best Cameraman to Ferenc Pap

- **OBJECTIVELY**, documentary (1977)

Directed by Pál Erdőss, camera: Lajos Koltai, László Vitézy
Balázs Béla Studio, black and white, 16 mm, 100 min.

- **RAIN AND SHINE**, feature (1977)
Directed by Ferenc András, written by Ákos Kertész, Géza Bereményi, Ferenc András, camera: Lajos Koltai
Cast: Erzsi Pásztor, Lajos Szabó, Imre Sarlai, Ildikó Pécsi, Anatol Constantin
Mafilm Hunnia Studio, colour
Prizes: Budapest: Hungarian Film Critics' Prize for Best Film, Prize for Best Cameraman to Lajos Koltai, for Best Actress to Erzsi Pásztor; Hyères: 'Humour Prize'; Karlovy Vary: Main Prize

- **ANGI VERA**, feature (1978)
Directed by Pál Gábor, written by Endre Vészi, camera: Lajos Koltai
Cast: Vera Pap, Erzsi Pásztor, Éva Szabó, Tamás Dunai
Mafilm Objektiv Studio, colour
Prizes: Cannes: FIPRESCI Prize; Chicago: 'Gold Hugo', Gold Plaque to Vera Pap for Best Actress; São Paulo: Audience's Prize, Critics' Prize; San Sebastian: 'Silver Shell" to director Pál Gábor; Budapest: Hungarian Film Critics' Main Prize, Best Script to Endre Vészi; Figueira da Foz: Silver prize; London: British Film Critics' Annual Film Award for Best Foreign Film; Oslo: Critics' Prize, Critics' Prize; Rome: 'David Donatello' Prize for Best Actress to Vera Pap, Best Producer to József Marx; Calcutta: Bengal Film Critics' Prize for Best Foreign Film of the Year; Cairo: Egyptian Film

Critics' Prize for Best Foreign
Film of the Year
- **THE STUD FARM**, feature
(1978)
Directed by András Kovács,
written by István Gál,
camera: Lajos Koltai
Cast: József Madaras,
Ferenc Fábián, Ferenc Bács,
Sándor Horváth,
Mafilm Objektiv Studio
and Dialóg Studio, colour
Prizes: Locarno: FIPRESCI
Prize, 'Ernest Artaria Prize
to Lajos Koltai;
Strasbourg: First prize;
Brussels: Audience's Prize
- **JUST LIKE AT HOME**,
feature (1978)
Directed by Márta Mészáros,
camera: Lajos Koltai
Cast: Zsuzsa Czinkóczi,
Jan Nowicki, Anna Karina,
Ildikó Pécsi, Ferenc Bencze
Mafilm Hunnia Studio, colour
Prizes: San Sebastian:
'Silver Shell'
- **AUTUMN WINTER
FASHION FOR '78-'79**,
commercial (1979)
Directed by Pál Sándor,
camera: Lajos Koltai
Mafilm Publicity Film Studio,
colour, 16 min.
- **A PRICELESS DAY**, feature
(1979)
Directed by Péter Gothár,
camera: Lajos Koltai
Cast: Cecília Esztergályos,
Pál Hetényi, Judit Pogány,
Lajos Szabó, János Derzsi,
Tamás Major,
Hédi Temessy
Mafilm Budapest Studio,
colour
Prizes: Budapest: Hungarian
Critics' Main Prize, Prize for
Best Actress to Judit Pogány,
Prize for Best Actor to Lajos
Szabó; Venice: 'Leone d'Oro'
in first film section

- **CONFIDENCE**, feature
(1979)
Directed by István Szabó,
camera: Lajos Koltai
Cast: Péter Andorai, Ildikó
Bánsági, Lajos Balázsovits,
Zoltán Bezerédi, Judit Halász,
Tamás Dunai, Ildikó Kishonti
Prizes: Berlin: 'Silver Bear' for
best direction to István Szabó;
Hollywood: Academy Award
nomination for Best Foreign
Film; Tokio: Foreign
Minister's Special Prize
- **STRATAGEM**,
documentary-feature (1979)
Directed by István Dárday,
Györgyi Szalai, camera:
Lajos Koltai, Ferenc Pap
Prizes: Budapest: Hungarian
Film Critics' Prize for Best
Script and significant part in
documentary-features to
Györgyi Szalai
- **THE GREEN BIRD
(Der grüne Vogel)**, television
feature (1979)
Directed by István Szabó,
camera: Lajos Koltai
Cast: Péter Andorai,
Hannelore Elsner, Krystyna
Janda, Johanna Elbauer,
Rolf von Sydow
Manfred Durniok Produktion
für Film und Fernsehen
(Berlin West)–SR
(Saarbrücken), colour
- **NOT YET THE DAY**,
feature (1980)
Directed by Lajos Fazekas,
camera: Lajos Koltai
Cast: István Bujtor, Mária Gór
Nagy, Gábor Koncz, Ági
Margitai, Ferenc Bencze
Mafilm Hunnia Studio-HTV,
colour
- **I DREAM ABOUT
COLOURS**, short stories
adapted to television feature
(1980)
Cast: Ádám Szirtes, Éva Vass,

Hilda Gobbi, Mari Törőcsik,
Péter Haumann, Iván Darvas
Mafilm Budapest Studio,
colour

THE AGE OF CONQUEST
(1981–1997)

- **TIME STANDS STILL**,
feature (1981)
Directed by Péter Gothár,
written by Géza Bereményi,
camera: Lajos Koltai
Cast: Pál Hetényi, Ági
Kakassy, István Znamenák,
Henrik Pauer, Sándor Sőth,
Lajos Őze, Jozef Króner,
Mária Ronyecz,
Ádám Rajhona
Mafilm Budapest Studio,
colour
Prizes: Budapest: Hungarian
Feature Film Festival, Prizes to
Lajos Őze, György Selmeczi,
Lajos Koltai, Péter Gothár,
Géza Bereményi; Cannes: Prize
of Youth; Chicago: 'Silver
Hugo'; New York: Film
Critics' Award; Taormina:
Second Prize; Budapest:
Hungarian Film Critics' Prize,
Prize for Best Director to Péter
Gothár, Prize for Best Camera
Work to Lajos Koltai;
Brussels: 'L'age d'or' Prize;
Tokyo: the Jury's Prize to
Péter Gothár, "the most
promising director"
- **MEPHISTO I-II**, feature
(1981)
Directed by István Szabó,
written by Klaus Mann,
camera: Lajos Koltai
Cast: Klaus Maria Brandauer,
Ildikó Bánsági, Krystyna
Janda, Rolf Hoppe, György
Cserhalmi, Péter Andorai,
Karin Boyd, Tamás Major,
Ildikó Kishonti

Mafilm Objektiv Studio-Manfred Durniok Produktion für Film und Fernsehen, colour
Prizes: Cannes: FIPRESCI Prize, Best Script to Péter Dobai and István Szabó; Budapest: Hungarian Feature Film festival, Special Jury Main prize, Prize for Creativity to György Cserhalmi; Agrigento: 'Efebo d'oro'; Cadiz: First Prize; London: British Film Critics' Award for Best Foreign Film of the Year; Channel Four: selected among the best four foreign films; Hollywood: Academy Award for Best Foreign Film; Milan: San Fedele Prize; New York: Prize of the 'Film Review' for Best Foreign Film; Rome: 'David de Donatello' Prize for Best Foreign Feature, for Best Director to István Szabó, for Best Actor to Rolf Hoppe; Sorrento: Italian Journalists' 'Silver Ribbon' Prize; Budapest: Hungarian Film Critics' Main Prize, Prize for Best Director to István Szabó, Prize for Best Actor to Rolf Hoppe; Warsaw: Polish Film Critics' Prize for Best Foreign Film

- **SCHWARTZ, ROT, GOLD (ALLES IN BUTTER)**, episode of a TV series (1982)
Directed by Dieter Wedel, camera: Lajos Koltai
Cast: Uwe Friedrichsen, Edgar Bessen, Gerd Böckmann, Hannelore Elsner
Norddeutscher Rundfunk, colour

- **THE PRINCESS**, feature (1982)
Directed by Pál Erdőss, written by István Kardos, camera: Lajos Koltai, Ferenc Pap, Gábor Szabó

Cast: Erika Ozsda, Andrea Szendrei, Dénes Diczházy, Júlia Nyakó
Mafilm Társulás Studio, black and white
Prizes: Hungarian Feature Film festival, Youth Prize, Prize for Best Actress to Erika Ozsda; Cannes: 'Gold Camera'; Kosalin: Diploma; Locarno: 'Gold Leopard', FIPRESCI-Diploma, Diploma of the Ecumenical Jury, Special Prize of the 'Cinema and Youth' Jury

- **GUERNICA**, feature (1982)
Directed by Ferenc Kósa, camera: Lajos Koltai
Cast: Ottilia Kovács, István Illyés, Tibor Szilágyi, Dezső Garas
Mafilm Objektiv Studio-ZDF, colour

- **KATZENSPIEL (Cats' Play)**, television feature
Directed by István Szabó, written by István Örkény, camera: Lajos Koltai
Cast: Maria Becker, Joana Maria Gorvin, Jane Tilden, Helmut Qualtinger, Loni von Friedl, Elisabeth Stepanek
Telefilm Saar-Saarlandischer Rundfunk, colour

- **BALI**, television feature (1983)
Directed by István Szabó, camera: Lajos Koltai
Cast: Winfried Glatzeder, Loni von Friedl, Michael Konig, Viola Sauer, Franke Singe, Sibylle Stern, Nicole Heesters, Roger Hübner, Milena Gregor, Béla Ernyei, Rolf von Sydow, István Szabó
Manfred Durniok Production–ZDF–ORF, colour

- **DER SNOB (The Snob)**, television feature (1983)
Directed by Wolfgang Staudte, camera: Lajos Koltai
Cast: Anne Bennent,

Heinz Bennent, Klaus Maria Brandauer, Gudrun Genest, Nicole Heesters, Sigfrit Steiner

- **COLONEL REDL I–II**, feature (1984)
Directed by István Szabó, camera: Lajos Koltai
Cast: Klaus Maria Brandauer, Hans Christian Blech, Armin Mueller-Stahl, Gudrun Landgrebe, Jan Miklas, László Mensáros, András Bálint, László Gálffi, Dorottya Udvaros, Károly Eperjes, Róbert Rátonyi
Mafilm Objektiv Studio, ORF, ZDF, Mokép, Manfred Durniok Produktion für Film und Fernsehen, colour
Prizes: Budapest: Hungarian Feature Film Festival: Special Jury's Main Prize, the Professional Jury's Prize for Best Camera Work to Lajos Koltai, for Best Sound Engineer to György Fék, for Best Screenplay to Péter Dobai and István Szabó, for Best Production Designer to Peter Pabst, the German Critics' Prize for Best Actor to Klaus Maria Brandauer; Cannes: Special Prize of the Jury; Sopot: Prize for Best Actor to Klaus Maria Brandauer; Valladolid: Special Prize; Ruel Maimaison: 'Silver Eagle"; Rome: Visconti Prize for István Szabó's life work; Budapest: Hungarian Film Critics' Prize, Prize for Best Actor to Károly Eperjes; Hollywood: Academy Award nomination for Best Foreign Film, Golden Globe nomination for Best Foreign Film; London: British Academy Award for Best Foreign Film; Warsaw: 'Gold Film' Prize for Best Foreign Film shown in 1986

- **ROOFS AT DAWN**, feature (1986)
Directed by János Dömölky, written by Géza Ottlik, camera: Lajos Koltai
Cast: Péter Andorai, György Cserhalmi, Katalin Takács, Dorottya Udvaros, Péter Haumann, Ádám Rajhona, Károly Eperjes, László Sinkó, János Bán
Mafilm Budapest Studio-HTV, colour
Prizes: Budapest: Hungarian Feature Film Festival: Prize for Best Camera Work to Lajos Koltai, Prize for Best Actor to György Cserhalmi

- **GABY – A TRUE STORY**, feature (1987)
Directed by Luis Mandoki, camera: Lajos Koltai
Cast: Liv Ullmann, Norma Aleandro, Rachel Chagall
Tri-Star Pictures, colour
Prizes: Hollywood: Academy Award nomination for Best Actress to Norma Aleandro, Golden Globe nomination for Best Drama Actress to Rachel Chagall, for Best Supporting Actress to Norma Aleandro

- **HANUSSEN**, feature (1988)
Directed by István Szabó, camera: Lajos Koltai
Cast: Klaus Maria Brandauer, Erland Josephson, Ildikó Bánsági, Károly Eperjes, Grazyna Szapolowska, Adrianna Biedrzyńska, György Cserhalmi
Mafilm Objektiv Studio, CCC Filmkunst, ZDF, Hungarofilm, Mokép, colour
Prizes: Berlin: Felix Prize nomination for Best Actor to Klaus Maria Brandauer; Hollywood: Golden Globe nomination for Best Foreign Film, Academy Award nomination for Best Foreign Film

- **HOMER AND EDDIE**, feature (1989)
Directed by Andrej Konchalovsky, camera: Lajos Koltai
Cast: Whoopi Goldberg, James Belushi
Kings Road Entertainment, colour
Prizes: San Sebastian: Golden Shell

- **GEORG ELSER (SEVEN MINUTES)**, feature (1989)
Directed by Klaus Maria Brandauer, camera: Lajos Koltai
Cast: Klaus Maria Brandauer, Rebecca Miller, Brian Dennehy, Nigel Le Vaillant
Mutoskop, colour
Prizes: Bavarian Film prize for Best Producer to Moritz Borman and Rainer Söhnlein; Fantafestival: Prize for Best Actor to Klaus Maria Brandauer; Berlin: German Feature Film Prize: 'Gold' to Klaus Maria Brandauer, 'Silver' to the film

- **DESCENDING ANGEL**, television feature (1990)
Directed by Jeremy Kagan, camera: Lajos Koltai
Cast: George C. Scott, Diane Lane, Eric Roberts, Mark Margolis, Vyto Ruginos, Amy Aquino, Ken Jenkins, Elsa Raven
HBO, colour

- **PERFECT WITNESS**, television feature (1990)
Directed by Robert Mandel, camera: Lajos Koltai
Cast: Brian Dennehy, Aidan Quinn, Stockard Channing, Laura Harrington, Delroy Lindo
HBO, colour

- **WHITE PALACE**, feature (1990)
Directed by Luis Mandoki, camera: Lajos Koltai
Cast: Susan Sarandon, James Spader, Jason Alexander, Kathy Bates, Eileen Brennan
Universal Pictures, Double Play, Mirage, colour
Prizes: Hollywood: Golden Globe nomination for Best Drama Actress to Susan Sarandon; London: British Film Critics' Prize for Best Actress of the Year to Susan Sarandon

- **MEETING VENUS**, feature (1991)
Directed by István Szabó, camera: Lajos Koltai
Cast: Glenn Close, Niels Arestrup, Erland Josephson, Moscu Alcalay, Macha Méril, Johanna ter Steege, Ildikó Bánsági, Dorottya Udvaros, Roberto Pollak, André Chaumeau
Warner Brothers, Fujisankei Communications Group, British Broadcasting, County Natwest Ventures, colour

- **MOBSTERS**, feature (1991)
Directed by Michael Karbelnikoff, camera: Lajos Koltai
Cast: Christian Slater, Patrick Dempsey, Richard Grieco, Costas Mandylor, F. Murray Abraham, Lara Flynn Boyle, Michael Gambon, Chris Penn, Anthony Quinn
Universal Pictures, colour

- **SWEET EMMA, DEAR BOEBE**, feature (1991)
Directed by István Szabó, camera: Lajos Koltai
Cast: Johanna ter Steege, Enikő Börcsök, Péter Andorai, Hédi Temessy, Erzsi Pásztor, Irma Patkós, Irén Bódis, Erzsébet Gaál, Zoltán Mucsi, Tamás Jordán, Gábor Máté
Objektiv Filmstudio, Videovox Studio, Audio Ltd., Manfred

Durniok Produktion, colour
Prizes: Berlin: 'Silver Bear',
Felix Prize for Best Screenplay
to István Szabó, Felix Prize
nomination for Best Actress to
Johanna ter Steege; Rome:
Italian Film Critics Association
Silver Reel Prize for Best
European Director of the Year
to István Szabó; Budapest:
Hungarian Film Critics' Prize
for Best Actress to Johanna
ter Steege
• **BORN YESTERDAY,** feature
(1993)
Directed by Luis Mandoki,
camera: Lajos Koltai
Cast: Melanie Griffith,
John Goodman, Don Johnson,
Edward Herrmann,
Max Perlich
Hollywood Pictures,
Touchwood Pacific Partners,
colour
• **WRESTLING ERNEST
HEMINGWAY,** feature
(1993)
Directed by Randa Haines,
camera: Lajos Koltai
Cast: Robert Duvall, Richard
Harris, Shirley MacLaine,
Sandra Bullock
Warner Brothers, colour
• **WHEN A MAN LOVES
A WOMAN...,**
feature (1994)
Directed by Luis Mandoki,
camera: Lajos Koltai
Cast: Andy Garcia, Meg Ryan,
Ellen Burstyn, Tina Majorino,
Mae Whitman, Lauren Tom
Touchstone Pictures, colour
Prizes: American MTV Movie
Prize: nomination for Best
Actress to Meg Ryan,
nomination for the Prize of
"the Most Desirable Man" to
Andy Garcia, Screen Actors
Guild Prize: nomination for
the Best Leading Actress to
Meg Ryan

• **MARIO AND THE
MAGICIAN,** feature (1994)
Directed by Klaus Maria
Brandauer, written by Thomas
Mann, camera: Lajos Koltai
Cast: Julian Sands, Anna
Galiena, Jan Wachtel, Nina
Schweser, Pavel Greco, Klaus
Maria Brandauer, Elisabeth
Trissenaar, Valentina Chico,
Rolf Hoppe, Philipe Leroy
Flach Film, Le Studio Canal,
Provobis Gesellschaft für Film
und Fernsehen, Roxy Films,
Satel Film, Thorsten Nater
Film, ZDF, ORF, colour
Moscow: Prize for Best
Camera Work to Lajos Koltai,
Special Prize, Andrei
Tarkovsky Special Prize
• **JUST CAUSE,** feature (1995)
Directed by Arne Glimcher,
camera: Lajos Koltai
Cast: Sean Connery, Laurence
Fishburne, Kate Capshaw,
Blair Underwood, Ed Harris,
Christopher Murray,
Ruby Dee, Scarlett
Warner Brothers,
Fountainbridge Films, colour
• **HOME FOR HOLIDAYS,**
feature (1995)
Directed by Jodie Foster,
camera: Lajos Koltai
Cast: Holly Hunter, Robert
Downey, Anne Brancroft,
Dylan McDermott, Geraldine
Chaplin, Claire Danes
Egg Pictures, Paramount
Pictures, PoliGram Filmed
Entertainment, colour
Prizes: US: Young Artists'
Prize, nomination for Best
Young Leading Actress to
Claire Danes
• **OFFENBACH'S SECRET,**
television feature (1996)
Directed by István Szabó,
camera: Lajos Koltai
Cast: Graham Clark,
Laurence Dale, Tamás Jordán,

János Kulka, Pál Makrai,
István Bubik, Sándor Sasvári,
Marcella Kertész, Géza Simon,
Melinda Major, István Szilágyi
I.S. L. Film GmbH, EuroArts
Entertainment OHG, black
and white and colour
• **MOTHER,** feature (1996)
Directed by Albert Brooks,
camera: Lajos Koltai
Cast: Albert Brooks,
Laura Weekes, Rob Morrow,
John C. McGinley, Paul
Collins, Debbie Reynolds
Paramount Pictures, Scott
Rudin Productions, colour
Prizes: New York: Film
Critics' Prize for Best Script to
Albert Brooks and Monica
McGowan Johnson, the
National Association of
American Film Critics' Prize
for Best Script to Albert
Brooks and Monica
McGowan Johnson, Golden
Satellite Prize for Best
Supporting Comedy Actress
to Debbie Reynolds;
Hollywood: Golden Globe
nomination for Best
Comedy Actress
to Debbie Reynolds
• **STEADYING THE BOAT,**
documentary (1997)
Directed by István Szabó,
camera: Lajos Koltai
Cast: Ildikó Bánsági, Péter
Andorai, Hédi Temessy,
Tibor Szervét, Irén Gyürey
BBC Scotland Ltd., ISL
Production, colour, 56 min.
• **OUT TO SEA,**
feature (1997)
Directed by Martha Coolidge,
camera: Lajos Koltai
Cast: Jack Lemmon,
Walter Matthau,
Dyan Cannon,
Gloria DeHaven, Brent Spiner
XXth Century Fox,
Davis Entertainment, colour

THE TIME FOR SYNTHESIS
(1998–2003)

• **THE LEGEND OF 1900,**
feature (1998)
Directed by Giuseppe
Tornatore, camera:
Lajos Koltai
Cast: Tim Roth, Pruitt Taylor
Vince, Melanie Thierry,
Bill Nunn, Peter Vaughan
Medusa Film, Fine Line
Features, colour
Prizes: Lodz: Camerimage:
Golden Frog nomination to
Lajos Koltai; Rome: David di
Donatello Prize for Best
Camera Work to Lajos Koltai,
Prize for Best Costumes to
Maurizio Millenotti, for
Best Director to Giuseppe
Tornatore, for Best Film
Music to Ennio Morricone,
Prize for Best Production
Designer to Francesco Frigeri;
Rome: Italian Film Critics'
Silver Ribbon Prize for
Best Costumes to Maurizio
Millenotti, for Best Director to
Giuseppe Tornatore, for Best
Production, for Best
Production Designer to
Francesco Frigeri, for Best
Script to Giuseppe Tornatore,
Special Prize for the original
style of the music to Ennio
Morricone; Berlin: Europe
Film Prize for Best Camera
Work to Lajos Koltai;
Hollywood: Golden Globe for
Most Original Film Music to
Ennio Morricone, Golden
Satellite for best Artistic
Management to Bruno Cesari
and for Best Set Design to
Francesco Frigeri, for Most
Original Film Music to Ennio
Morricone

• **SUNSHINE,** feature (1998)
Directed by István Szabó,
camera: Lajos Koltai
Cast: Ralph Fiennes,
Rosemary Harris, Rachel
Weisz, Jennifer Ehle, Deborah
Kara Unger, Molly Parker,
William Hurt, James Frain,
John Neville, Miriam
Margolyes, David de Keyser,
Mari Törőcsik, Kathleen Gáti,
Vilmos Kun, Péter Andorai,
Péter Halász, Gábor Máté
Alliance Atlantis, Serendipity
Point Films, Kinowelt, Robert
Lantos production, Bavarian
Film, Telefilm Canada, ORF,
colour
Prizes: Europe Film Prize for
Best Actor to Ralph Fiennes,
for Best Camera Work to
Lajos Koltai, for Best
Screenplay to István Szabó and
Israel Horovitz, nominated for
Producer of Best Film to
András Hámori and Robert
Lantos; Canada: Genie Prize
for Best Producer to András
Hámori and Robert Lantos

• **MALENA,** feature (2000)
Directed by Giuseppe
Tornatore, camera:
Lajos Koltai
Cast: Monica Bellucci,
Giuseppe Sulfaro, Pietro
Notarianni, Gaetano Aronica,
Matilde Piana, Luciano
Federico
Miramax International,
colour
Prizes: Hollywood: Academy
Award nomination for Best
Camera Work to Lajos Koltai

• **TAKING SIDES,** feature (2001)
Directed by István Szabó,
camera: Lajos Koltai
Cast: Harvey Keitel, Stellan
Skarsgård, Birgit Minichmayr,
Moritz Bleibtreu,
Oleg Tabakov
Little Big Bear Production
and Partners, colour
Prizes: Europe Film Prize
nomination to Stellan
Skarsgård; Mar del Plata: Prize
for Best Director to István
Szabó, for Best Camera Work
to Lajos Koltai, for Best Actor
to Stellan Skarsgård

• **MAX,** feature (2002)
Directed by Menno Meyjes,
camera: Lajos Koltai
Cast: John Cusack,
Noah Taylor, Molly Parker,
Leelee Sobieski
Lions Gate Films, colour

• **THE EMPEROR'S CLUB,**
feature (2002)
Directed by Michael Hoffman,
camera: Lajos Koltai
Cast: Kevin Kline, Emile
Hirsch, Embeth Davidtz,
Rob Morrow

• **BEING JULIA,** feature (2002)
Directed by István Szabó,
camera: Lajos Koltai
Cast: Annette Bening,
Catherine Charlton, Maury
Chaykin, Shaun Evans,
Jeremy Irons, Juliet Stevenson,
Michael Gambon
Myriad Pictures, colour
Prizes: Hollywood: Golden
Globe for Best Actress in a
Motion Picture (Musical
or Comedy) to Annette
Bening, Academy Award
nomination for Best Actress
to Annette Bening

ACKNOWLEDGEMENTS

I am pleased to express my gratitude to all those who helped in the writing of this book. First of all, I would like to thank Lajos Koltai for sparing his time at every possible and impossible moment. Valuable help was also given in depicting his career by a remarkable group of colleagues, from György Illés to István Szabó. A special thank you is due for ensuring my working conditions during shooting to the producer, András Hámori, the managing director of Hungarian Cinema Ltd., Lajos Szakácsi, and the production manager, Endre Sík, as well as many others participating in the production of the film. I cannot list by name all the colleagues whom I have not only known for more than three decades, but with whom I have also been involved in film-making. Thank you all.

I am grateful to Katalin Gál, the Director of Vince Books, for persuading me to write this book, the somewhat weighty financial burden of which is born generously by the publisher alone. I thank those working for Vince Books for their professional approach and expertise. They have helped to publish a book which is unique among works on Hungarian cinema.

Finally, I would like to thank Imre Kertész for accepting my request amidst his diverse engagements and giving me the opportunity, during a long conversation, to hear, in the interest of authenticity, his viewpoint about the film *Fateless*. Furthermore, I am grateful that I could learn about the story of his acquaintance, creative cooperation and friendship with Lajos Koltai, and could ask about aspects of what is usually left out of interviews made with him, namely what role cinema has played in his life.

PHOTOGRAPHS
(page numbers)

Typeface: Sabon and Interstate
150 gm Euroart matt paper,
five-colour impression, flexi-cover